# Giving a Voice to the Child Left Behind

Navigating the unspoken grief of parental suicide in childhood.

By Maddie Roberts

## *Disclaimer*

This book is based on the personal experiences and views of the author.

Identities have been protected and events described for the purpose of providing information and knowledge for anyone who has been through or is supporting someone who has been through a similar experience.

These are the personal views of the author and advice should be taken with that knowledge in mind.

Please see chapter, "Charities and support organisations", for expert guidance and information.

The content of this book may evoke emotional responses, please be mindful and reach out to appropriate professionals and services if needed.

## About the Author

Maddie's passion for helping people naturally led her to pursue her career as a nurse.

A job she loved but when her children came along, she wanted to dedicate her time to being a full-time mum.

When her son was diagnosed ADHD and autistic, he struggled with mainstream education. Finding support in the online community Maddie found a new passion for advocating for her son and other families facing this difficult situation.

Maddie and fellow SEND parent Susan Liverman campaign to stop fines and prosecution for families with children who can't, not won't attend school.

Change.org Parent petition No school fines has gained almost 300,000 signatures as parents support and share lived experience.

Seeing how sharing lived experiences empowers people and makes them feel less alone, Maddie decided to write and share her inner child perspective of losing a parent to suicide.

In hope that this insight helps adults supporting children with this grief and to find relatability in the isolation we feel.

# *Foreword*

Losing a loved one at any age can be one of the toughest experiences we face in life, but to lose a parent as a child is one of the most shattering and life-altering experiences any individual can face. In this book, Maddie Roberts will take you on the rollercoaster of emotions that surround loss as a child and how difficult it can be to live with the aftermath of a loss as your life progresses, with an honest, raw and experience-led story that pulls no punches.

Sadly, Maddie lost her father to suicide a number of years ago, at a time when the stigma around men's health and male suicide was even stronger and more widespread than it is today. Maddie's father passed away in 1993, only 26 years after suicide attempts were decriminalised, and only 10-15 years after catholic churches started to allow suicide victims to be buried on their church grounds. As a whole, the United Kingdom has always had a strange relationship with mental health and with suicide and it is this relationship that has made it so difficult for people to deal with suicide and loss.

There is so much of Maddie's story that I personally relate to. I too lost a parent at a young age and the pain of this loss was difficult to deal with. I found different family members dealing with this in different ways. My father had severe addiction issues and had brought a lot of trouble to my family's door over the years, meaning that some family members had a reluctance to talk to me about my father and his story, and to fill in the blanks that I needed to fill in after such a profound loss. Listening to her story, I felt a bond with Maddie in that I too was looking for someone to give me a hand to hold and to give me answers to questions that burned away at me for years. This is why Maddie's book and mission are so hugely important to me and to our charity, finding relatability underpins everything that ANDYSMANCLUB aims to do. When some men are going through difficult life circumstances, they feel alone in their problems and as though the world and life has picked a fight with them specifically. By listening to the problems of others and finding a common ground, people can feel less isolated and as though their problems are more usual than they initially thought.

If this book can reach one person who needs it at the right time, then it will be a job well done! Enjoy and please reach out to any of the amazing services listed if you need to.

Lucas Whitehead
ANDYSMAN CLUB

# Dedication

For my children Mikayla, Harleigh and Vinnie, who brought unconditional love back to my life.

I love you and promise never to stop my healing journey to be the best mum I can.

I've made mistakes, I am growing and learning daily with your guidance.

Our little Roberts family, who love and accept each other for who we are.

My husband Leigh. Through our difficulties you have always remained by my side, I'm thankful for that. I love you.

To my readers:
I'm a great believer that people come in and out of our lives for a reason. Some to help us grow and learn, others to teach us life lessons, that, at the time may feel painful, but on reflection teach us a great deal about life.

I'm grateful for those that have crossed my path and tried in some way to understand parts of my life experience. For those that have arrived and not been able to understand but have remained and helped me to grow and heal.

Within this book, I hope to bring you an honest and open insight into the confusion and isolation I felt, having lost a parent to suicide in childhood and share the knowledge I have gained.

I hope you can take something from this book to help you or a person you are supporting to connect and feel less alone in the complexity of suicide grief.

Much love,

Maddie x

## *For Dad*

Hidden pain and struggles
You hoped would go away
They didn't die with you
On that tragic day
They live in those who knew you
Your daughters and your wife
Who continued to miss you for all their life
Some say that you were selfish
I know this isn't true
You must have felt so hopeless
Life just too hard for you
If only you had found the strength
To speak and talk it through
People would have helped you
Maybe they felt it too
30 years have passed
Our love forever lasts
There are no second chances
No time to start again
If only life worked in that way
We would ask for you to stay

Leon Wood 1964 - 1993

# Contents

# Introduction

*Sunday 6th June 1993*

*It's a bright sunny Sunday morning. I'm 11-years-old and wake up at Nan and Grandad's house, as I often do on a weekend. Today is no different, it's car boot sale day.*

*My cousin Jemma and I run round all the stalls. Pocket money clutched in our hands, excitedly searching for a new toy to buy. We love getting to run round the stalls before the gates open. Rummaging in boxes to find the best stuff as people unload their cars.*

*The oddness begins as family members start to arrive; Uncles and Grandad, they never come to boot sales.*

*From the distance I watch them huddle around our stall, hugging one another. Intrigued to why a family gathering is happening, I run over to them. An uncle hugs me, but there is a strange atmosphere, no one is speaking, their faces almost expressionless. They have been crying their eyes are red and puffy. I don't get a chance to ask any questions. Nan grabs a large cardboard box from the car, places it on the ground, her arm sweeps the content of the table into the box. There is lots of glass and breakables, in the silence we hear them smash.*

*"Get in the car girls, we are leaving." Nan instructs.*

*It's not a tone of voice Nan has used before; we do as we are told and get in the car.*

*No opportunity to ask why we left suddenly as the car gets a flat tyre. Nan cries and tells Grandad to change it now. There is a tension, the adults are stressed and upset. The tyre sorted we begin our car journey, clueless to where we are headed. Grandad parks at the village hall. Family gatherings take place here, it is fun usually, but Nan's unfamiliar voice continues.*

*"Stay in the car girls, we will be back in a moment."*

*It's the first opportunity Jemma and I get to talk.*

*"What do you think is happening?" I ask Jemma.*

*"I don't know," she shrugs.*

*Of course, I know she doesn't know, we've been together the whole time.*

*A strange feeling comes over me as my aunt appears out the village hall. Grandad's arm around her, comforting her.*

*"This must be something bad."*

*"I think someone has died," I voice my fears to Jemma. "Maybe it's a relative that lives far away, we don't see often."*

*I try to make sense of this confusion; my thoughts turn to what could have happened.*

*"Maybe Great-grandparents that live at the seaside?"*
*"We don't really know them, they live far away, but the grown-ups would be sad if they have passed away."*

*"One uncle has epilepsy, he goes to hospital sometimes when unwell, maybe he is poorly?"*

11

*We don't get long to talk; Nan and Grandad are back in the car.
Silence returns as we drive away.*

*We arrive at an aunt and uncle's house. It's down a country lane,
the houses have large front lawns. A peaceful area.*

*The magnitude of the situation starts to sink in. There are relatives
everywhere. Some sitting alone, some in little groups. They are all
crying. Hugging. Smoking a cigarette.*

*They look lost in their own space on the lawn.*

*Jemma and I are parted.*

*I'm stood at the bottom of the driveway. Grandad tells me he will
get Mum and to wait here for her.*

*Mum walks towards me down the long driveway, she is crying too.*

*I hope she will hug me, tell me what has happened and reassure
me everything is okay.
I don't know that what she is about to tell me will change my life
forever.*

*Mum speaks through her tears, her voice shaky, it's difficult for her
to speak,*

*"I am so sorry Mad, there was an accident this morning and your
dad has died."*

*The world seems starts to spin around me, it's like I am underwater. I cannot quite hear what is being said. I can see she is talking, but I can't hear any noise.*

*My mind racing… Dad... I haven't even thought about Dad this morning. I have not questioned where he was when family arrived at the boot sale. I hadn't even realised he was missing…. I just thought he was at home with Mum. Where they always are while I'm with Nan and Grandad.*

*"Why hadn't I looked for him? Why hadn't I thought of him?"*

*I hear the words, "No… no… no" projected out of my mouth, the words out of my control. They become more distressed and louder. I can't stop the tears streaming down my face.*

*The word 'no' stops, it's abruptly replaced with, "You are lying, it's not true."*

*Crying so much, it's hard to breathe, I'm shouting at Mum in anger.*

*"Why would you lie?"*
*"Why are you saying this?"*
*"What sort of accident?"*
*"A car crash?"*

*None of this makes sense.*

*"Why wasn't he at home with you?"*

*He was meant to be home safe, home when I return from my sleepover like he always is.*

*I try to walk towards the house. I want to find him. Mum holds me back.*

*"Let me go, he's in the house, isn't he? With everyone else?"*

*"Let me go… I want Dad, I want to find him and hug him," I beg Mum. "Please let us go in the house and find him."*

*Mum holds her arms out to hug me, comfort me… I hit her, shout for her to let me go, get off me, let me find him and stop lying to me.*

*My body starts to shake, I feel weak, I need comfort and reassurance.*

*I know Mum isn't lying, I know she wouldn't do that, I can't be angry with her.*

*I surrender and fall into her embrace. Hold her tight as she gently whispers, "I'm sorry he really is gone."*

*Once calm, the instinct is to run. Run away from the house, from people, run and find somewhere to hide… but I can't.*

*I look down to my feet… I still have my roller boots on. The roller boots that just a few hours ago I was whizzing around on carefree and having fun with Jemma at the boot sale.*

*This memory already feels like a lifetime ago.*

*What a ridiculous time to have roller-skates on, I think to myself.*

*Sat on the ground I remove them, I will never have fun on these stupid things again, nothing is going to feel like fun again.*

*I know my childhood is over.*

*I don't feel like a child anymore. The world doesn't feel the same. It doesn't feel real, the world, my surroundings, even family sitting around.*

*I do not feel safe, this world doesn't feel safe. I don't want to be here anymore. I can't say 'I want to die' but I want to be with my dad.*

*Grandad says he will take a walk to the phone box. Situated at the end of the lane.*

*"Can I come?" I ask him. I need some space; the adults are not talking just crying. I don't know what I am meant to do. I love spending time with my Grandad, he agrees I can come too.*

*He picks up the phone, ready to dial the number, he asks me to step away so that he can talk. I want to be good; I want to do as he has asked, but curiosity for the truth takes over. Today has been full of confusion and it's making me feel uneasy. I've never experienced this before and it's not a nice way to feel.*

*I hear him say hello to the person on the phone, I quietly creep closer behind the phone box where I am sure he can't see me.*

*It's the hospital.*

*"He informs them that he needs to identify a body."*

*"His son. Aged 29 years."*

*"He said a word I haven't heard before; I don't know what it means."*

*"Suicide."*

*Grandad is a kind man, whilst we are alone walking back to the house I know if I want to find out the meaning to this word suicide, I need to ask now. I must tell him the truth, that I listened to the phone call. To express that I am sorry, I didn't do as he had asked, I did not move away from the phone box.*

*He gently crouches down next to me and explains in the kindest way he can, it means he had taken his own life.*

*I'm eternally grateful and thankful for his honesty. I think about if/how/when or who would have broken this news to me if he hadn't now. Would I have found out some other way? Would I have been told in weeks/months or even years to come?*

*His open, honest and gentle explanation makes me feel I am treated as a grown-up. It takes some of the confusion away knowing the truth.*

*It must be difficult for him to break this news; he is patient and kind. He asks if I have any questions.*

*I don't have any that I am able to get out in words, but inside my head begins a lifetime of questions. Many that will remain forever unanswerable.*

*We walk back to the house as an ache develops deep in my heart.*

*"My Dad left me. He left all of us."*

*"Didn't he love me? Enough to stay?"*

*"I loved him. I loved him the world. I would never want him not to be here"*

*"He was not perfect, but he was my dad."*

In writing this book, I'm doing something I've not done in 30 years. I'm giving a voice to my inner child, the child that was left behind.

Allow her to tell her story, her thoughts, experiences. To do what never came naturally, give her love, kindness and compassion.

This is an invitation into a space I've never shared before.

Picture it as the loft space in my brain. Where she has lived, surrounded by boxes with 'memories' written on the side. You can probably blow the dust off the top of them.

In the far corner there is a tornado of emotions, frustrations, and isolation spinning.

Through this journey of healing, we will explore them, talk openly about them, release them from the tornado that has caused great exhaustion carrying alone.

This is to validate my inner child and set her free.

## *Not a typical introduction…*

More of a welcome.

It's taken a lifetime to say these words.

"I am enough."

For years I tried to fit in, connect with people for who they are, not who I am. Confused about the world, who I am and where I fit. That stops now. Written authentically and unmasked, without shame of feeling differently to others. I'm brave enough to accept that life experiences and traumatic events have shaped who I am and how I experience life.

"I am me and that is enough."

By the end of this book, I hope you will be saying this too.

You absolutely are enough.

You have searched for a book looking for insight and knowledge around suicide grief, which makes you an incredibly brave and valuable person not only to yourself, but those you are supporting.

If you are feeling like you are failing or not coping as well as others:

*\*\*\*You are doing your best and looking for ways to help yourself and others\*\*\**

That is enough.

You are doing your best and that is all anyone can ever ask for.

I'm sorry that you too have felt the indescribable pain that the loss of someone by suicide leaves behind.

Through validating and healing my inner child's experiences, I have found forgiveness and healed my inner child; we have found peace.

Finally ready to move forward in life without the heaviness of pain and grief.

Processing childhood trauma has been lonely and painful, but I've been doing it through life without even noticing. Deciding to share this journey with you, those who have suffered alone in this grieving and for those trying to understand and support children facing this heartache, to let you know there is hope that healing from losing a loved one by suicide is possible. (Something I never thought I would say/write/feel)

Loneliness and confusion are the hardest parts. I write this, not as a book of 'strategies or the theories of grief and trauma' (there are many of those from the professionals), but as a friend, as someone inside these pages who wishes to help you feel less alone. To share insight and what I've learned along the way. There are others out there that do understand and finding those connections is so important.

Some of you might be looking for the 'magic' chapter. The "How do I stop the pain and make it all better?"

I will save you the time in searching, there is no such chapter I'm afraid.

I wish there was, it would be the one and only chapter. I could pass you the magic wand.

There's no quick fix, no jumping to the end of the journey where life feels real again.

There will be a 'new you' after the loss of a loved one. There is no turning back to life before this experience happened, sadly; there is a future though, it's confusing and overwhelming, but that's okay. Connecting to others who have felt this, when we support and share our experiences, it allows us to realise it is normal and part of the healing process.

It cannot be rushed; it will happen when you are ready and know, this will take time to heal from.

Each human experience is different and unique, I can't tell you how your young person is feeling or thinking or even what they personally need. I'd like to try to help you understand what they could be experiencing by connecting you with them and with yourself.

You know them better than anyone else, or at this moment in time you might feel you don't know them at all. I certainly didn't know who I was, what I felt, or what would help, but what I do know is the lack of a bond or connection with someone was the worst part.

Suicide leaves a gaping ache that is complex. Supporting yourself or someone to heal needs a different type of love and understanding. Kindness and consistency.

Listening and validating difficulties, pain and struggles allows us to individualise the support required.

Remove the expectation of 'following what society thinks the healing process should look like.'

Look at things from a unique perspective can support us to find our own ways to heal.
Develop a bond and heal together with others around you. The hurt is a crucial part of the healing (but also the part we all want to skip).

The silence and awkwardness around suicide massively contributed to the hurt continuing for so long. We must be able to feel the hurt and express our pain to enable us to let it go.

The intention of sharing this is not to upset people, if it brings out those emotions, we begin to let go of what we have been holding on to in our hearts. We have emotions we have yet to let out, it's okay to cry, to release those tears. Even writing this I feel the emotions in my chest, the way I used to fight with all my strength to hold it in and not cry.

*I would like to highlight the importance of supporting a child after suicide loss. If a scaffolding of support isn't provided during childhood, it may lead to a life of confusion and unhealed trauma.* However, it's never too late to start building those connections and talk. To hold space and help support the process of healing. Maybe they are waiting for someone to offer that space.

This book represents the things I wish I found a voice to tell Mum and adults around me.

It's the experiences no-one knew about. Things that could have helped other children and people understand me better. My childhood has passed, unfortunately there are no second chances at life, we can't start again, but we can move forward and share the knowledge we have gained.

Mum passed away 10 years ago, she can't read this book. In ways I am grateful for that. I would never want to hurt her or make her feel guilty. It's not any part of the purpose in sharing this experience. I loved her, she was my best friend, towards the end we had conversations about childhood. She knew she hadn't always got it right; she was sorry for that. I knew she tried her best, this traumatic event, losing her husband, the father of her children, was unexpected. No-one prepares us for that, there is no life manual on how to cope. You simply do your best to get through. She knew I loved her and her me, that was all that really mattered when we said our final goodbyes.

I will pause here…

For anyone reading who feels guilty, a failure or that they haven't done enough for a child or their children.
Take a moment to be kind to yourself, be gentle and compassionate. In a life-changing moment, you have done your best to survive and carry on.

There is absolutely no judgement within these pages.

No judgement for things we didn't know how to cope with.

Finding freedom and peace has taught me not to judge my past self, we did what we had to, to get up and make it through each day somehow.

Search for self-kindness that you too have managed to do that.

## Realisation for the need to heal and the tornado in my head

I wake up on 9<sup>th</sup> May 2023, just turned 41 years old.

Picked up my phone, checked my messages and through habit go to look at social media.

"No… I'm not going to do that"

Recent events on social media, I have found myself feeling vulnerable and unsure who to trust.

"Where do I turn and who can I trust?"

"Why do I feel vulnerable?"

"Why do I not see red flags that others talk of?"

"What causes me to feel unable to trust?"

"What makes me so worried about the rejection from others?"

The only person that can answer these questions is … me.

I have trauma, big trauma I have never fully understood. Never felt ready to address the complexity of it or where to begin.

How can I pick the little scab off this wound to try to process my vulnerability and fears in adulthood?

The only way is to rip the whole thing off and go way back.

Back to the very beginning.

I inhale the biggest breath I am able to, hold it for as long as possible, and slowly exhale.
This is overwhelming, I'm giving myself permission to heal.

I'm not entering this chapter of my life naïvely, but I've said it out loud now. I'm ready to start this process, there is no backing out, or pushing it aside for another day.

I'm not fantastic with big words and meanings, others may be able to articulate themselves in more eloquent terms. That wouldn't be truthful of me, that is another step in accepting myself, I am good enough. I am me, that's all I can ever be, and it's time to embrace that.

I'm not highly intelligent, but that doesn't mean I'm not a genuine human being, who thinks deeply and cares fiercely about people.

I am sure I would benefit from massive amounts of therapy and professional intervention, but I cannot afford that financially… or catch a break from the mad crazy family life that I call home.

That's okay, I've made peace with that, I'm going to have to be creative and find my own way. When the house is quiet, when I can hear myself think, I can concentrate on writing and processing.

There has been what I describe as a tornado spinning in my head. A gale-force wind, the confusion pushes these emotions around fast like a tornado, which sucked in each feeling, claiming experiences in its path. Experiences, memories, conversations.

Spinning in the back of my mind.

Always there, always spinning, I learnt to block the noise out. Put it behind a door, not think about it or deal with it. The tornado is big, the whirlwind strong and powerful.

Subconsciously draining energy. Like an energy-sapping source that doesn't get switched off.

The book will reflect on experiences, this time with compassion and love for my inner child. Be the adult I guess she always needed.
It wasn't her fault, she deserved love and protection.

She should not have held this all in alone for so many years.

Show acceptance and reassure her it's okay, she did her best. It's time to pick apart the emotions and set them free.

"What did these events teach me?"

"What do I need her voice to tell others?"

Deal with the tornado, one piece at a time.
Of course, I have thought about these experiences, but I've opened the door up and thrown it back into the tornado and told myself... "not today".

We need validation of the pain we feel in a way that is true to us.

You could say the closest people to this situation would be my siblings, they shared this life. Their feelings, memories and pain will be different to my own.

Professionals and society may tell us to all deal with our trauma in a similar way, but surely that doesn't always work for everyone.

Writing and truly listening to the thoughts I come to the realisation…. I am the one that knows how to heal my wounds.

Today is that day, I finally feel ready.

"Could it be the tragedy that shocked me at a young age?"
"Could this be the reason it has taken this long to feel ready?"
"I don't know, but I'm pleased to have arrived."

From a drawer, I pick out a necklace I had made years ago, from its little pouch.

A small pink love heart pendant with two small forget-me-not flowers, one curl of my mum's hair and a little of her ashes.

It has never been worn, but I figured one day I would need this, for comfort, for strength, maybe guidance even.

Round my neck it goes for the first time.

The front garden is full of beautiful bluebells. I love them, like tiny fairy feet dancing in the wind and a glorious scent.

I pick a large handful, I'm as ready as I will ever be. Time to drive to a place I've not been in years…

The cemetery to visit Dad's grave.

Before I visit the cemetery, I pop to my auntie's.

Tell her I'm off to the grave, she looks at me almost with guilt and says, "it is very overgrown Maddie."
She continues, "Nan and I have ordered cleaning stuff, we are going to clean it up."

I reassure her, not to worry, keeping it clean and tidy isn't the responsibility of just one person. We are all guilty of not tending to it. Many family members never go there. Never visit, the pain too much still. Maybe some don't think of him as there. They may have other ways to remember him.

"That's okay, it shouldn't be forced upon any one person to take it on as their role."

I've walked through these heavy black metal gates many times in my life, the familiar noise of them squeaking as they are pushed open.

Much of the time it is silent. Just the calming, "coo-coo" of the pigeons in the distance.
It's certainly a sound I associate with being here.

Every step gives a crunchy sound underfoot, the gravel path leading to his place of rest.

This time is different, the most difficult visit I've ever done, today I'm ready to relive and process the experience.

To go back through time, I allow the memory to come to mind.

*I'm 11-years-old, it is the day of the funeral.*

*I have been given a choice: to attend or not.*

*Mum says I can choose to remember him as his was and not have the memory of him being buried or I can go if I wish.*

*My decision is not to go to the funeral. I don't like the idea of him in a coffin alone. I don't want to see his coffin put in the ground.*

*Mum promises to take us to the grave after the funeral. When the others have left, so we can say goodbye.*

*I feel involved for the first time. It's the first time I've had control of the craziness that has unfolded around me.*

*Mum talks to me like a grown-up, about how she felt losing her mum when she was young. It brings some comfort, not that she felt sadness too, but that I am not alone in these feelings. She explains that she had visited her mum after she passed, the adults told her it would be like her mum was sleeping.*
*Mum speaks honestly about what it was like, her mum didn't look like she was sleeping. When she kissed her goodbye, she felt cold. I feel sad she has this memory, but I'm grateful she shares it with me, because now I need to decide about Dad.*

I can feel she is trying to protect me and guide me.

"If you would like to remember Dad as he was and the good times that's okay. If you want to come to the funeral, I won't say you can't. He was your Dad."

I can't get my head round hearing people say, "he was". It's so final. He isn't coming back. Hearing him spoken about in past tense makes my heart hurt.

I think about this for a while, she is right, I want to remember the Dad I loved and admired, not the memory of a coffin with his body being placed into the ground. If I do attend, I don't trust myself that I won't beg them not to put him in the ground.

Mum keeps her promise and takes us to his grave after the burial.

She's 27 with three young daughters, aged 11, 5 and 3.

Mum sits on the grass next to his flower covered grave, I notice the other graves are old, they don't have the mound of freshly dug dirt laying on top.

I wonder how long the other graves have been here. I think of the people buried in the ground.
"Who were they?"
"What were their lives like?"
"When and why did they die?"
"Did they also decide to take their own lives?"
"Do they have children left behind?"

My thoughts are heavy on life and death.

*Trying to figure out what causes death.*

*Someone to just suddenly stop being.*

*I'm struggling with the fact one day we are just not here. It scares me that there is absolutely nothing we, the people left behind, can do about it. We cannot change it once it has happened, we cannot stop it from happening.*

*These thoughts are too big. I haven't had thoughts like this before. It feels unreal, I don't have the words to express this. What I do know, is that I will never see life the same again.*

*I look up and see my school playground. My friends and other children are playing tag, kiss chase and kicking a ball around. Laughing and joking. Things I would normally be doing with them.*

*They look like they are having fun…. Thoughts come into my head; I cannot stop them, as hard as I am trying. I don't like them, these thoughts I can't control.*

*"Why don't they feel the hurt I'm feeling right now?"*

*"Why isn't this their Dad?"*

*I want it to be them, I want them to be me. I don't want this, "Why can it not be someone else?"*

*I don't like what my brain is thinking, my heart knows I don't mean these things, I don't want any of my friends to feel this, or any other child.*

*I have never experienced this feeling of not being in control of thoughts, they are just there in my head. My brain is making me feel very sad, alone, and I know I cannot say these things out loud. People will think I am horrible. No, these thoughts must stay in my mind.*

*I wonder if I will ever have those feelings again? Freedom, fun, laughter? It doesn't feel like it right now.*

*In the days after Dad's death, the adults have been telling Jemma and I to go and play. They say things like, "We are talking grown-up things."*

*"Go and play. Have some fun."*

*I don't want to play; I don't feel like having fun. Whatever that is meant to look like now.*

*I need to be close to them, the grown-ups.*

*I need to feel safe knowing they are in the same room as me. Where I can keep a close eye on them, nothing can happen to them if I can see them. They can't just disappear and not come back.*

*I fear that Mum will leave us too. I look at her differently, my mind races and panics …*

*"What if she leaves?"*

*"Where is she going?"*

*"What is she doing?"*

*"Could she get hurt, or worse, die?"*

*Will she leave us too? To be with Dad, she is so sad and crying all the time for him to be back.*

*"I'm just going for a wee, Mads, I will be back in a minute", she says when she leaves the room. In my mind I question, "Might this be the last time I ever see her?"*

*"What if she doesn't come back in the room?"*

*It doesn't feel safe for her to be out of my sight. I'm powerless to ensure she is always going to come back when I am apart from her. I can't stop this worry. I can't change it. What good would it do to tell Mum, or any other adult? They cannot undo what has been done either.*

*"Who else is there to blame?"*

*"You, Dad. You did this to us all."*

*I stop watching the children play and look around to remember I'm at the cemetery.*

*Suddenly I'm scared with my thoughts, I need Mum to hold me, make me feel safe from these thoughts.*

*Running back to Mum, I sit down next to her on the grass at his grave, snuggle myself into her as tight as I can. She is warm and feels like a safe place, protected under her arms.*

*The words cannot find a way out of my mouth, but an intense feeling …please never leave me this way Mum is deep in my soul. Never leave me, I love you, I need you more than anything in the world, but my voice is silent.*

*As I cuddle up to her, I hear her gentle sobs as she speaks to his grave,*

*"What am I going to do now? How am I going to live without you?" Holding her tighter is all I can do.*

*I don't remember seeing grown-ups cry before this, and certainly never lots of grown-ups crying. They don't seem to stop. When Mum is alone, when they are all together, this is all they have been doing. I can see they are hurting, but I don't know what to do to make them feel better.*

*"Will they ever stop crying?"*

*The grave is surrounded by flowers.*

*Flowers made to look like his favourite things, a pool table, a motorbike… the hardest one to look at, the one that stands out the most to me blue and white flowers that read*
*DAD.*

*This is his final place of rest, this is his home now, where he will stay forever.*

*That word. Dad. I will never get to call him that again.*

*Dad, the love and bond that is gone.*

*I want him back; I want this not to be true. "Why my dad? Why did he have to leave us like this?"*

*"Didn't he love me, us, his daughters, his wife enough to stay?"*

*"Was I, were we not good enough to stay for?"*

*"Maybe if I'd been better behaved, done as I was told more, would he have stayed?"*

*"Didn't he love us, his children?" He decided one day he had enough of this world.*

*These questions are on a loop in my head, they go round and round, day and night. Nights are the worst when I'm trying to get my brain to stop with the questions and try to sleep. It's impossible, in the silence of the night they become louder. I can't find any answers and the adults don't have the answers. You are the only one that can answer these questions, and you are not here to ask.*

*My heart hurts watching mum cry, she looks broken, I've given up counting how many cigarettes she has smoked. We seem to have been sitting here forever.*

*I don't think she wants to leave his grave, leave him here and carry on without him. Now he is buried, it feels so final, once we leave here, we must find a new way of living without him. None of us want to leave him alone, in the ground, we want to take him home with us. Not his actual body, but him, we want him back to take with us. Somehow, I know this emptiness is going to last forever, I won't stop wanting him, his love, his cuddles and the way he made me feel safe. The deep ache of sadness and disbelief is growing stronger, because I will never have a Dad for the rest of my life.*

# In the beginning

*In May1982 I enter this crazy place called The World.*

*My Mum, Debbie, 16 and my Dad, Leon, 18.*

*They don't tell anyone they are expecting me, Mum hides her baby bump under baggy jumpers. A huge, unexpected arrival for everyone else. Mum had known tragedy of her own when her mother passed at 31 years old.*

*Mum had taken on a caring role to her younger sister and brother, while her father worked to provide for them.*

*Mum talks fondly of her mum and their bond. She sounds like a beautiful caring lady.*

*What a lovely Nan she would have made.*

*I wasn't planned, but they wanted to keep me. Maybe the fear of them being so young prevented them from announcing the pregnancy?*

*They work hard and save their wages, and at 18 and 20 years of age they buy their first house. A little two-up-two-down cottage in a small village, they are so proud of it. They never try to hide the fact we have so little. In every way, no furniture, not much money, but we have our own little home. It isn't all sunshine and happiness; my Dad does have a temper, and his moods can change fast. He works long hours as an electrician; it can't be easy having a child and responsibilities so young.*

*My grandparents live in a village not far from our house.*

*I spend a lot of time with them.*

*Playing out in the massive garden and going on long walks with Grandad.*
*Nan and I spend our time growing vegetables in the garden and shedding peas from their pods. We water the flowers, mow the lawn and love watching spring come to life.*

*We pick Grandad up from work at lunchtimes, he always has a bag of his favourite sherbet pips in his jacket pocket, and of course I am allowed to pop my hand into the bag and take a handful for the ride home.*

*At 5-years-old, I become a big sister to Charley.*

*When Charley is 2-years-old, Mum is pregnant, and it is time to move house. Our family has outgrown the little two-bedroom cottage. The new house is bigger and on the outskirts of the village.*

*We have our own bedrooms. It's like a bungalow, everything on one floor, apart from Mum and Dads' room it is the only room upstairs.*

*I pick my room; it has a door that leads out to the huge back garden. The garden is amazing and has lots of trees to climb.*

*It feels strange, Mum and Dad's room all the way down the long corridor, through the living room and up the wooden stairs to their bedroom. I don't mind too much, as my sisters' room is here next to me. I don't like being alone at bedtime, in the dark, it's scary.*

*At night-time when I'm lonely, I go into Charley's room scoop her up and bring her in my bed. Turns out having a little sister isn't so bad after all. She is warm and snuggly. I love her and do feel guilty when she gets told off for keep getting in my bed at night. She says, "but Mummy, I didn't get out of my bed."*

*I don't want to be getting in trouble, we do enough of that doing other things.*

*The house has a conservatory, where Mum breeds her cats. We play with them all the time. We love all the kittens and the fun they bring.*

*At the bottom of the garden is a huge shed. This is my Dad's favourite place, full of work tools and always a half-finished motorbike.*

*He spends hours in there, I don't really understand why, but he loves taking motorbikes apart and putting them back together. I love being in here with him, handing him tools and feeling an important part of this bike fixing.*

*In 1990, our baby sister Izzy is born, I'm almost 8-years-old now and Charley is nearly 3.*
*Izzy comes home in a tiny yellow and cream outfit; she is like having a real-life doll. Mum is cross with Dad, he is always doing jobs around the house, always on the go, needing to be doing a project. Mum's face when she brings Izzy home, Dad and I have knocked the wall down in the living room. It looks like a builder yard she says, dust everywhere, she is furious. It is rare that Mum is cross, on this occasion I don't understand why, because Dad and I had great fun.*

*It doesn't stop him from doing crazy jobs around the house though. Mum despairs as he impulsively decides to start new projects at home.*

*We cut one of the trees down from in the garden, as it falls it just misses the conservatory by inches, Dad and I stand giggling. I enjoy it when he does crazy things like that, it is exciting he always lets me join in.*

*He isn't always easy to live with sometimes he gets angry and shouts. Especially if something goes wrong when he is trying to fix it. He always makes me feel loved though and I feel special because I get to fix things with him. I go in the car when he gets his work materials, Charley and Izzy are too young, so I get his attention all to myself and I love it.*

*I think music makes him happy; there is always music playing, even when he is in a bad mood Queen goes on full blast.*

*At parties and barbeques Freddie Mercury is always played. Dad loves a get together he is the one to arrange them. Barbeques are my favourite times. I get excited when he plans these. He has four brothers and a sister, they have partners. There are more cousins than I can keep count of. I like this new house, it's fun here. The music plays loud and the grown-ups chat and laugh for hours. Us kids make our own fun, mud pies and the rope swing tied to the tree keep us well entertained.*

*I love Freddie's songs too and spend hours with massive headphones on listening to songs. Laying by the big old-fashioned stereo. The headphones have a wire connected, so you cannot move far. The disc box has a paper in with all the words to the songs, it makes it easy to sing along. We find it so funny when Charley is singing, "...another one throws their guts".*
*Mum laughs so much… it's … "Another one **bites the dust**"."*

*I'm surrounded by family and love time with them.*

*I especially love sleepovers at different relatives' houses and staying up late with cousins having midnight snacks. Watching movies and playing video games, what is there not to love?*

*My cousin Jemma and I spend lots of time together. We feel more like sisters than cousins.*

*Our Mums are sisters and always together, we live in the same village. Jemma like me has a younger sister Kirsty, she and Charley are a bit too young to join in with our games.*

*Jemma is quieter than my loud talkative self.*

*We have fun together, I love being at Jemma's house, it feels like home from home.*

*We get to spend time with her grandparents too. They own a pig farm not far from where we live. My uncle works on the farm. While the adults are busy, we get to see the pigs and baby piglets. I just love them the piglets are too cute.*

*It takes time to get used to the awful smell, but getting piglet cuddles makes it worthwhile.*

*One day there was a piglet to the side of the pen, it wasn't moving and when I touched it, it felt cold.*

*"What is the matter with it? Why isn't it moving?"*

*Jemma's Grandad comes to see what trouble we are getting up to, he knows us well.*

*We ask him what happened to the piglet, he says, "Sometimes they don't all make it. It's part of life I'm afraid."*

*"What do you mean, 'didn't make it'?"*

*"He died." Jemma has more experience of this than me and explains there is a pig grave.*

*"But what happens to them then?"*

*"Well, they stay there forever, they go to Heaven." We agree.*

*We continue to play, but this is now a question in my mind, "What is Heaven and why do some piglets die and not others?"*

*I feel sad for a while, but I understand it is part of life.*

*Back to the farmhouse, we wash our hands eat some food and talk with Jemma's Nan.*

*She is lovely and always makes me feel she is happy to see me, just as much as she is to see Jemma. When it is time to say our goodbyes, Jemma and I look at each other and giggle… we know what is coming next.*

*Jemma's Nan squeezes us tightly, kisses us on the head and stands at the front door to wave goodbye, always with, "See you another day."*

*I love that saying, she makes us feel she really does want to see us another day.*

# The night before life changed forever

*We are at the village hall, in the tiny village where Grandad still lives. Him and Nan have separated now, but it still holds many happy memories. The village hall is where the family comes together. Weekends, Sunday afternoons playing pool, nights of discos, karaoke nights, wedding receptions, birthday parties any celebration… they take place here. Always. Most of the family will be here, aunts, uncles, grandparents, cousins. Extended family. Us kids run wild and usually end up pushing two chairs together to make a bed, falling asleep by the end of the night. I do not do it often, I don't find sleep easy at home in my own bed, so I don't feel sleepy with all this excitement and noise going on. The little ones do, pulling everyone's coats over them as blankets. That is what these days and nights are all about, it is normal life. Tonight is no different, Dad always sings Queen or Freddie Mercury songs on the karaoke. He enjoys singing Crazy little thing called love and having his favourite beer, Special Brew.*

*We are having fun, Dad is in his playful annoying mood… rubbing his stubbly beard on my face, tickling us and making us laugh. We have a car boot tomorrow, so Nan says it's time to go. We always get up early to go set the stall up. We say good night to everyone I give Dad a hug and say goodnight, along with all the other family.*

*We walk down the big steps that lead to the car park and open the car door to get in. Dad follows us out to the car, this seems a little strange, he doesn't usually follow us out to the car.*

*He gives me a huge hug and says, "I love you."*

*"Yeah, I know you just told me that indoors." I reply.*

*"I really love you and I want you to be good for your Mum." he continues. This seems strange to me. Is he drunk? I think to myself, I'm going with Nan not Mum.*

*I'm confused. "Why is he telling me to be good for Mum?"*

*"I love you too Dad." I say as we get in the car. He walks up the big steps to go back inside, he turns and waves us off, shouting, "Love you" as we drive away.*

*"I think he might have had too many beers tonight." I say to Nan, still trying to figure out why he said be good for Mum.*

That is my last memory of Dad. Waking up the next day to the news he had taken his own life, that conversation made sense. That was his goodbye to me. Unknowingly that was my final goodbye to him too. He had known he was leaving, I guess telling me to be good for Mum was some kind of message he wanted me to have.

Even before he died, I hadn't been an easy child. I had terrible meltdowns and often would have temper tantrums, as they called them. I didn't really know the cause of why I often felt so frustrated and angry. Mum would wait until he got home from work and ask him to talk with me. I had a different relationship with him, I think he could be the more understanding parent, he listened when I tried to explain why I had not been good for Mum. Somehow by just being with him and having him listen helped to calm my mood.

Was that the meaning behind him telling me to be good for Mum?

I guess I will never know, but in my mind that was his way of trying to make things easier for Mum after he was gone.

Family Portrait 1992

# How did he die?

I never wanted to make people sad. If it upset or aroused emotions in people, I somehow felt responsible for that. To not talk about it felt like I could protect others from these emotions. It provided protection for me from their reaction, questions, or judgement. With time and maturity, I learned that other people's reactions to my loss are not my responsibility. If it brings up emotions in them it shows that they feel our sadness too and they care.

That is okay, having empathy and sharing pain isn't something to be ashamed of or shied away from. It can help to bring connection with others. They may have trauma and loss they haven't processed and healed from. Pushing those feeling deep inside and not finding a way to release them means the hurt has been carried longer.

I think that not wanting sympathy and sadness was a coping mechanism my inner child found. If people were kind or acknowledged my hurt and pain it would make me cry.

In hindsight that is what I needed to release the pain and cry, to let it out and connect, but of course I didn't know that then. Instead, I held it in.

As I was growing up, well-meaning people often said, "Don't cry."

"Who did this benefit?"

The person that feels uncomfortable to see your tears and pain.

Grab a box of tissues and let those feelings free. Encouraging and allowing time to cry isn't a bad thing. We shouldn't feel that it is weakness, that we are not coping, rather simply it has become too difficult to hold. Some people said, "I feel so sorry for you."

Pity was not a feeling that felt comfortable. I realise now they were of course well meaning, but as a child/teen I didn't see it that way. Therefore, it caused a barrier to me being able to open up and talk to them.

Maybe if they had been able to acknowledge the difficulty rather than say they felt sorry for me,

"That must be really difficult" or
"That's a lot for you to go through."

To my mind, one of the fundamental differences in telling people your Dad has died of natural causes or an accident, rather than suicide, is the reaction people have when hearing it is to suicide.

To say your Dad has taken his own life, brings shock and an awkwardness of people not knowing what to say. It always felt like a topic not to be spoken about. A topic other people didn't want to discuss.

If someone has passed of natural causes, it's sad of course, people have empathy for that loss. When it is suicide, it seems to catch people off guard and brings a shocked response.

I will discuss the question how did he die?

The impact it has on life interactions. It is difficult to explain just how much anxiety this simple question produces. The anxiety that follows you around on a day-to-day basis.

"It seems like a simple question, right?"

"An innocent question?"

Maybe from a place of genuine interest of the person asking? Human nature of being curious?

The problem is and always has been... It's a difficult question to answer for those left behind after suicide. It brings up lots of emotions and vulnerability.

It can lead to anticipation and uncertainty of how the person asking will react.

"Am I prepared for the shocked look on their face?"

"Am I prepared for the possibility it triggers their own experiences?"

"Am I prepared to lay my vulnerability and personal circumstances bare to this person?"

Suicide is a personal experience.

As a child and in my early teens, it quite simply was a question I dreaded.

Meeting new people was not something I enjoyed because the conversation would inevitably lead too.

"What are your Mum and Dad's names?"

"What do they do for a living?"

Normal, innocent small talk and get-to-know each other.

*I dread this situation, this topic of conversation. Playing amongst friends on the playground, they are laughing and chatting about their mums and dads. My mum's Polly and she bakes cakes... my dad is called Steve; he drives a fast car.*

*I try and change the subject, my mind racing about what I can say. What can I change the subject to?*

*"What is everyone's favourite colour?" Randomly plucking questions out of my head.*

*My head is spinning as I start to feel this panic in my stomach rise. I feel shaky and like I want to cry, but I hold back the tears as I don't want the attention and questions that brings. I don't want to cause a fuss and for everyone to be looking at me. If only there was a pause button… someway to change this or make it stop.*

*There isn't.*

*"What are your Mum and Dad's names?"*

*I knew this was coming and I have no idea how to handle it. No-one has ever told me I don't have to talk about it. I want to try and be friends, join in with their games and conversation. However, I'm not laughing and having fun talking about my parents.*

*My Mum name is Debbie… my voice wobbly and tears sting my eyes, hesitation is holding back my words, I'm getting prepared to say this out loud… my Dad's name was Leon.*

*It upsets me to say his name. It reminds me he has gone. He is in the past. He left and in moments like this I realise I will have to relive that moment all my life. A flash back to mum telling me he was gone.*

*"Oh" their faces look confused. "Was? What happened to him then?"*

*"He passed away." I don't like saying it out loud. It makes it more real somehow. When I am just in my head it feels safe, I don't have to answer questions, and I can pretend that maybe it has all been a bad dream.*

*"Oh… how did he die?"*

*"He took his own life." Sometimes I use the more factual approach, "by suicide."*

*******SILENCE*******

*I don't know what I want or need, I don't like the uncertainty of how they will react. It is out of my control. I don't know how to handle this and it's my life, I can't expect other children to know what to say.*

*"The one thing I do know time and again… I don't want this to be my life."*

*"I don't want this to have happened to my Dad, my family or me."*

51

*"I can sense each of them hoping someone will say… something."*

*Sometimes they say sorry. Sometimes they say sorry they asked. I don't want them to be sorry, they only asked a question, they haven't done anything wrong. They couldn't know what I was going to tell them, it wasn't their fault. Sometimes they ask me outright, "Why did he do that?" I feel they are trying to understand, but I do not understand it myself. I do not know why he did it. Even when I do ask the grown-ups why… they don't know either. Not knowing why and not being able to answer their question my thoughts wonder off to a deep place. Thinking, searching my mind again in the hope I might one day stumble across the answers in there. Those uncontrollable thoughts are back again, I can't quieten them… "Why did he leave?"*

*Standing here in the playground I find myself back to thinking about the unanswered questions. I hadn't been thinking about this until they had started talking innocently about parents.*
*I can only describe it like a can of worms. When I'm not thinking about it, they are tight in the can and when someone asks a question, the lid comes off and there are worms everywhere. Long after the conversation has finished, I'm still scrambling around trying to get the worms back into the can. When the conversation arises, I get that unsafe feeling again, like when Mum told me. I want to run and hide, be left alone. No-one understands what this feels like, and as much as I want to explain it, I can't find the words.*

*"I feel so alone without someone who knows what this feels like."*

*The fast change of topic comes, I can feel it and we don't know how to talk about it, so we don't. The atmosphere changes and I wish we could go back before this conversation had happened and I wasn't thinking about all of this.*

*I watch as they run off and continue their games and playing. Talking about their parents again.*

*"I don't fit in."*

*I miss my old life; I want Dad and family life. I'm drained from this situation … But I know it is only a matter of time before it will arise again. Maybe hours, maybe weeks, maybe even months, but this conversation will happen again, and I dread it.*

*At times I can see the thought of, "I wish I never asked" pass through their minds. Of course, once it has been asked it is too late to take back, the only way forward is to continue in this uncomfortable situation.*

*"They probably believe they are doing the kindest thing for me by changing the subject."*

*"They possibly feel they are protecting me from the hurt by not talking about it."*

*After the conversation ends, my mind doesn't rest. Thoughts and emotions whirling round my head. I cannot bring my focus back to the here and now. I am unable to focus on what the conversation has changed to. As the adrenalin starts to calm in my body, I try to imagine a life where this isn't the answer I have to give. I'm left feeling slightly sick and holding the tears in my eyes, alone, with this ache inside my body. I wish someone could put their strong arms around me, hold me, fill me with their strength, so I don't feel I always have to be strong and just deal with it.*

*Over time and with more experience, I try different ways of answering the question.*

*"He was unwell, and he passed away."*

*That isn't a lie. His mind was not well, I do not fully understand what this means, but it's what the grown-ups say.*

*This answer brings further questions ...*

*"Had he been ill for a while?"*

*It feels like it is prolonging the inevitable...having to tell the truth.*

*I try to find ways to make it less painful for me. Struggling to get the words out I say,*
*"I don't know my Dad," or*
*"I don't see my Dad."*
*It feels I'm not acknowledging him; it just doesn't feel right to me somehow. I feel guilty, it isn't a lie, but it also doesn't feel truthful.*

*"Maybe I tell the truth to find a connection and validation."*

*When people seem shocked by me telling them, I can't open about it and talk more. I don't really know why, but I just can't.*

*When people change the subject, it feels like they do not want to talk about it, so I don't try.*

*As I enter my late teens and early adulthood, the question never seems to get any easier. If anything, it hurts more. It is a part of my past that I cannot escape from, memories I relive with each new person I meet.*

*When these conversations arise, the environment often isn't right to start deep conversations. There is always a feeling of trust issues, talking to people you barely know, you don't know if they will become part of your life. Sharing a personal life experience with someone in passing, about suicide a topic so many shied away from talking about.*

*Not processing or healing from the trauma of a parental suicide in childhood leaks into interactions with the people you come to meet in everyday life. How can you possibly talk about it comfortably even if just briefly in passing, if you have not resolved the confusion in your own mind?*

*I find myself trying to talk to someone else about the experience, the experience I haven't healed from. For most of the time you try to forget or suppress these feelings, but then unexpectedly they are forced to the surface and take you by surprise. Leaving you quite literally without words. I hate the feeling of being placed on the spot, people waiting for you to reply. I just want to be me, without sharing what has happened. You meet people, pass quick chit chat, have brief friendships with, for me there was always anxiety that it could be brought up at any point.*
*It was nice to have some connections to people that didn't know or ask. I found the initial sharing of this the hardest part, after people knew I felt able to relax a little, become friends and continue with the friendship/relationship without it being something I was worrying about. Not everyone we meet of course become close friends/acquaintances, no-one is going to remember every detail about your life or each conversation you have. Its information others can forget (sometimes I think lucky for them, for me this will*

*never be forgotten) time passed and they ask again... "What is it your Mum and Dad do?" "What do your Mum and Dad think about so-and-so." I remind them of what had happened, in this situation it doesn't feel too bad for me, as id already told them once, I feel sorry for them as they feel guilty. "Oh, my goodness, I'm so sorry, I forgot."*

Don't get me wrong, I did want to talk about it, but I guess I felt I needed it to be on my terms. When I felt comfortable in the environment, when I had gotten to know them well enough to want to talk about it.

I did have friends that I talked to, shared memories, tried to describe what it was like. I must admit as supportive as they were, or however good their listening skills were, I just never found a true connection with anyone. I knew they couldn't understand what I had been through, try as they may, imagining such tragedy and loss is a difficult thing for anyone to try and do. Plus, to add to the mix, these were children too in the early days, being 11 years old, few children would want to picture the loss of their parent in such a way. Adults had a hard enough time trying to get their heads round it, so expecting children too was unrealistic. What I'm trying to highlight is, that without a connection/bond with someone who also had lived experience of losing a loved one to suicide made the world a very lonely and isolating place.

Being young children and trying to navigate friendships of course meant none of us knew how to deal with the topic. That is part of the importance of society learning that's it is okay to talk about suicide and not knowing what to say or do.

There is no right way to bring it up in conversation, to comfort someone after the loss, be it immediately or many years after the death. Hiding it away, silence, treating as an off-limits conversation, because of the fear of upsetting someone or getting it wrong, is not an option if we genuinely want to support someone in their healing.

This may be confusing, I've written about wanting to talk about it, not wanting to talk about it, wanting people to be interested, but not wanting to be placed on the spot.

This is the complexity of suicide for those left to grieve, I'm sure for much of the time I didn't know what I wanted. As confusing as that may sound to read, it was even more confusing as a child. What I really needed was someone to guide me through the whirlwind of emotions in my head.

Unfortunately, I wasn't given tools or emotional support to answer this difficult question.
I returned into the world to navigate this situation alone.

It was a taboo subject 30 years ago and still is today. I do believe if it was discussed more openly and freely it wouldn't have been so hard to navigate friendships and interactions in life.

So, I am ready to talk openly and honestly about the suicide of a parent.

I hope by being vulnerable enough to share, it will help others in supporting children.

Help others like me, who may have similar experiences and are holding on to a lifetime of grief and loneliness, to connect and to know you most certainly are not alone.

Give hope that in starting these conversations we can make suicide a less taboo subject and instead of being something we shy away from talking about, because of the pain and fear, we can learn to talk and support those left behind from suicide with care, compassion, connection and open communication.

Thinking about it now, I realise that I hadn't accepted it or made peace with it and didn't like the way it could become part of conversations in daily life without me having any control over it.

## *Things to consider*

Maybe if I had therapy, support, the opportunity to process what happened, I may have been empowered (given permission, even) to reply with something like:

- "This is a difficult subject for me, could we talk about it another time?"
- "Thank you for showing an interest but I don't feel like talking about this now."
- "It's a difficult subject for me, my Dad has passed away, please can we leave it there and I will talk to you when I feel ready?"
- "It's too painful for me to talk about right now."
- "Here doesn't feel like the right place to talk about this. Would you like to talk about this with me somewhere quieter?"
- "I would like to talk to you about this, I just feel I can't today."

# Gossip and children's ears

As adults, we come to realise humans seem to love a bit of gossip. What is happening in other people's lives and sharing details that have been heard. Many seem to think of this as harmless chit chat. The words and information shared in these conversations can be so hurtful and damaging to those whose lives are the subject of this gossip. Often not factual and with little regard to the impact it can have on the individual and their families, especially when the topic is the loss of a loved one through suicide.

Thirty years ago, suicide was a very uncommon thing to hear about, so living in a small village community I can only imagine the shock and impact it had when people heard of Dad's passing.

The ripple effect of tragic news. There may have been an inquest into his death, I clearly remember over hearing mum on the phone to the papers saying that she wasn't happy with what had been printed. Explaining she had children who could read. I never did read anything or see any newspaper report, it was different back then, she could protect us to a certain degree by hiding newspapers.

My heart hurts for those that face loss of a loved one to suicide now, as with the advent of social media and internet, it is not so easy to protect children from seeing and reading. It adds a certain powerless feeling again, that what happens privately is published for others to read. It's both hurtful and harmful to have such a personal circumstance written about for all to see. It takes away privacy and the right to share information as and when a family feels ready to.

They say little ears hear everything and they sure do.

We must be careful in the conversations about tragic situations and be mindful of little ears that are listening.

*We have been staying with my Aunt and Uncle since Dad died. This house that has always felt like a home. I'm happy Mum has adult company. Jemma and I are always together, this is a huge comfort to me. I don't want to be alone and when we are together, we don't have to be talk, but I just like that she is with me. I can talk to her about the thoughts in my head, well most of them, not the bad ones that keep coming without my control. I don't talk about these with anyone. We share her bedroom and at night if I'm scared or upset, I gently wake her and talk. Bless her, she never complains or tells me to go back to sleep, she listens. We are trying to make sense of this situation together.*

*The funeral hasn't taken place yet. Father's Day is soon, so Jemma and I go to the village shop and to buy a card. Mum says she will put it in the coffin. It feels strange this is the last Father's Day card I will ever get to give him. My heart aching, this really is goodbye. It is freeing that the adults have given us some independence and freedom to go shopping. Although, we think the adults have sent us to get us out of their hair while they continue the adult talk.*

*We walk into the familiar village shop and start to look at the card selection. It feels strange buying a card for someone that isn't here, he won't get to see it or read it. Looking at all the cards with Dad or Daddy written on, just reminds me I won't ever have a Dad again. My mind is wondering deep off into this thought when I hear the man behind the till start talking to another person in the shop.*

*I'm not deliberately trying to listen; I don't care much for chatting right now, but in the silence of the small shop it is all we can hear.*

*I don't remember his name, so will use Fred.*

*The conversation begins…*

*"Isn't it awful?"*

*"Have you heard?"*

*"Poor old Fred was out on his early morning dog walk on Sunday and found a body."*

*"He is in a right old state, bless him, you don't expect that on your morning walk."*

*"You know anything about them?"*

*"Well, I heard he was only 29 and up until recently lived in the village. The family has not long moved to the next town."*

*"It is heart-breaking he has left three young daughters behind."*

*I'm frozen to the spot, my heart is pounding, a lump in my throat, tears filling my eyes. I look over at Jemma, we both know this is Dad they are discussing. I am one of those daughters.*

*This familiar feeling is starting to rush through my body, wanting to run, wanting to hide. Wanting this to not be happening, to somehow just disappear from this all. I want to shout at the men in anger, that's my Dad and my family you are talking about. You have no right to be talking about this, it's none of your business. New questions race in my mind,*

*"A man on a dog walk?"*
*"What was Dad doing there?"*
*"How had this dog walker found him?"*
*"How long had he been there, dead, for before the man found him?"*
*"Did the man try to save him?"*

*The list of unanswerable questions is filling my mind.*

*I wonder if I will get in trouble for hearing their conversation if I speak out?*
*Will I get told off for being rude to them if I question them?*

*My head is spinning again, the underwater feeling is back, they are still talking, but I can't hear the words. Panic is taking over, no-one here to tell me what to do. I feel sick, how can everyone else know things that I don't even know. How has this even happened? I've just come for a card and now things are making even less sense.*

*I grab any card, pay the man at the till and get out of the shop.*

*Once outside we decide that this is something we need to tell the adults. There is a safe feeling returning to Jemma house. This experience has confirmed why I feel unsafe in the outside world. A least when at home I'm protected from other people's gossip.*

*I write my card and place it with a single red rose on the kitchen side. It sits amongst the other things people have brought round to put in his coffin. You can't see the worktop, its overflowing with items. Special Brew beers, they were his favourite. Packets of cigarettes, photos, envelopes with goodbye letters from family and friends. Records of his favourite music bands, of course lots of Queen and a pool cue. Mum comments that if it carries on like this there will be no room in the coffin for him. It warms me to know he was obviously so very loved, everyone wanted to put something of meaning in there with him to take on his way.*

*I can't help but think why he didn't know this. How come he didn't feel all this love people had for him? Why did he have to leave all these people who are now crying and heartbroken he is gone? I wish all this love had been enough for him to stay.*

*We return to the family home for a visit; to collect some belongings, I think mum wants to get something to put in his coffin. As we walk into the house for the first time after his passing, it feels strange, and not like home without him here. His things are scattered all over the house. We have only lived in this house for 6 months and it hasn't got that home feel to it. I didn't like moving to this house and blamed it for making me move school. Leaving the village school and friends behind. I didn't particularly like this house. It didn't help I was being bullied by a girl at school because she made it clear I had taken her friends away from her. The other girls had welcomed me and tried to help me settle.*

*I hope I don't have to go back to that school now that Dad is not here. I would like to go back to the village and my old school. Remembering the men chatting in the shop, I start to realise the village isn't going to be same, people are talking about Dad and our lives. Maybe the friends at the village school know now too.*

*I don't want to return to this house and that horrid school. I also don't want to face the friends in the village school if they are all gossiping too. How I wish this would all go away, nowhere feels comfortable.*

*Dad's shoes are on the floor from the last time he took them off, never to be worn again. These trivial things, a pair of shoes, bring such big emotions inside. Not able to express this sadness I look over to Mum, there is a jumper thrown over the back of the sofa, she picks it up, smells it, hugs it tight and begins to cry again. I'm pretty sure she takes that jumper with her; we leave not knowing if or when we will return to this house again. It's all so confusing, like living in the unknown of what the future holds. For now, we return to my Aunt and Uncle's house, they have told Mum we can stay for as long as we need to.*

# Things to consider

- The child might feel they want to be involved with decisions and conversations; this doesn't mean to say they have to be involved in all situations/discussions but make time for inclusion and hear their contributions and thoughts.
- Offer for them to be involved, "We are talking about funeral arrangements, would you like to be involved?" "Is there anything that is important to you that you would like us to do/say?"
- If the child feels excluded and confused by what is happening, they may try to overhear conversations to gain insight and knowledge.
- Allowing time for open and honest conversations. So that they can ask questions about what is confusing them or anything they feel like they might like to know.
- Being honest that you might not have the answers, but that it's important to you that their worries are heard and shared.
- Rather than giving the information you think they want to know, ask them questions about what they would like to know. Answer honestly, but with age-appropriate language.
- Give choices which allow them to feel they have some control in what's happening to them.
- "Would you like to be involved in the conversations?"
- "Would you like to attend the funeral?" Prepare them for what it might be like, reassure them that it's okay if they don't feel ready. Don't force them to feel they have to do/say things if they are not ready to. Offer support and be there for them if they need you. Remind them that they are not alone.

- Remove expectations or pressure. For example, "Well, your brother/sister is going, so you should."
- Is there anything special they would like to keep as a reminder of their parent? Any special memories that could be a keepsake. Do they want to keep them now or are there things that could be kept and given to them when they are older?
- Give space/time to be alone if they need it. If they feel they don't want to be alone at night for example, could they sleep in a room with someone else in the early days for reassurance and comfort?
- Be mindful that they may overhear gossip outside the house/at school. This might be very confusing and hurtful to them. Let them know it is okay to tell you if this happens.

# Myth busting… just a child

There seems to be a myth: they are just a child.

They will get over it.

They will forget in time.

Children are resilient and strong.

Maybe people think that if they don't mention the loved one who has passed, a child will somehow magically forget them and the fact they have died.

Do adults over time simply forget a loved one after they pass? No.

Why does society presume this would be the case for children?

Yes, our minds are young, we have a lot of developing to do, but that doesn't mean that the death of a loved one is any less painful or as devastating as it is for an adult. Simply because we are children doesn't mean our pain and memories disappear and fade in a different magical way. Leaving a child to try and unpick and process a death because it is believed they will forget? Not in my experience, this was complete nonsense. In fact, quite the opposite, it remained unprocessed and unhealed… I can assure you never once forgotten. Just packed up and carried as an emotional burden.

A burden, carrying a traumatic event until well into adulthood. Finally finding the courage to unpick and speak out about what it was like.

Is this because adults don't have the knowledge and skills to support a child? Is it because the enormity of supporting a child with this huge life changing trauma. Is it that this is what society, and previous generations have taught us? If we don't talk about it will just go away?

Is it that suicide is such a taboo topic, one of which people shouldn't talk about or the stigma that causes guilt and judgement? A hidden secret amongst those families that experience it.

Maybe because they honestly believe if they don't talk about the event, it will somehow be deleted from a child's memory?

I've had people ask….

"You were so young, just a child, do you remember your Dad?"

The fact no one talked about him through fear of upsetting me, made me feel I had to cling onto every detail and memory my brain could. At times it felt like he had never existed, to me, his daughter, I wanted to hold on to everything I could. He did exist. He did live. He was part of my life. I would replay memories repeatedly in my mind, so they didn't fade, to ensure his memory stayed alive to me. That meant the good and the painful. I was part of him, he was part of who created me. How could I forget him?

Maybe it is why I can author a book with such clear thoughts of him, the emotions, and the confusion. When I've written from my inner child's perspective, it's been like handing her the microphone and giving her permission to speak. Saying it's time for you to have your voice now, it's okay to talk about him. It's been incredibly freeing and has connected me with her. She has lived in there holding on to these memories for all this time, waiting for someone to want to hear her experience.

People talk about you being the only person that can save you, to be there for yourself; no-one else can fix you.

How can we expect this to be true of a child when so many adults find this nigh-on impossible to do?

I understand this statement now. I became the adult I needed as a child. I looked at her with care, compassion, and love. In many ways, for the first time in my life with real admiration, because she survived this. She kept us alive and did her absolute best in a life-changing situation without the guidance and support she desperately yearned for. I'm so incredibly proud of her. It is time now for adult me to acknowledge what she went through was tough.

A lack of feeling protected, no-one said, "I'm here, I can help you with these difficult feelings." No-one that stayed as a constant in her life. No-one that committed to that role, except her.

I wonder now if that role and responsibility was simply too much for the adults. They had their own grieving to do. The difference was, they were adults. They had other life experience. They may have lost others to death, they would have been aware of suicide, even if they hadn't known anyone who had died in that way, they knew what it was. More to the point, they had fully developed brains; as children, ours are still developing. I as a child had no concept that someone could take their own life, that people do that. Until it was my Dad. One of the people in life who is your protector, gone not only by death, but a self-inflicted death.

Let that sink in for a moment and then ask the question,

"Do you really believe that a child will just get over this or forget over time?

It wasn't as though I had fallen over, cut myself badly, would heal and forget the experience. It baffles me now when people talk about children's resilience or that they will grow up and forget what happened.

Nobody asked me to write this book, to share my lived experience, which came naturally and through my own choice.

However, I do wonder if that is because no-one has ever asked…

"What was it like for you to lose your Dad to suicide at such a young age?"

"Maybe they didn't want to upset me?"

"Maybe they didn't know how to deal with the answer?"

"Maybe they thought it might upset me?"

I can see clearly now that it was/is a major part of why my experience has never felt validated.

If someone can be brave enough to ask the question and be honest; that they don't have the answers, they can't fix it or make it all go away, but they can listen, that would have been the best support they could have ever given.

To just listen, not give advice, or tell you it is going to get easier, one day it will not hurt as badly.

Simply offer validation for the pain, hurt, and confusion.

"It's okay to be angry at him."

"It's okay to love him still."

"It's okay to not know how you feel."

"It's okay to feel confused, for these feelings and emotions to change daily. Even minute by minute."

"It's okay and natural that it might feel like that now, in months, in years, maybe even forever. That is the complexity to losing a parent to suicide."

"It's okay to feel lost, lonely, different to how you did before this happened. I am here if you feel scared of these big emotions, we can work through them together."

"The feelings and emotions you are experiencing are valid."

You can't force a child to talk, what you can do is build a bond, gently (and consistently) remind them you are there when they are ready.

Adults might tell us its helps to talk, but first we must find an adult we can trust. That is incredibly difficult when one of the most trusted people in your life has just abandoned you by suicide. It's almost as if the adults who are left around you must gain your trust, which can only come from them being a consistent presence in your life.

Saying "I'm here for you" doesn't feel genuine if they don't prove that by consistently actually being there.

Saying "I'm never going to leave you" doesn't feel believable.

Death has been forced into our lives now, no-one can prevent death from happening. Car accidents happen, incurable diseases happen, heart attacks happen. They are not controllable and once death has entered a child's life it can heighten anxiety that other loved ones in our lives will also die. They will die. We will all die eventually. This might not be by suicide, but as children we are now very aware of life and death. Its unpredictability. Life is unpredictable. No-one can promise us they will never leave.

Things that sound more reassuring include,

"I'm not planning on leaving you,"
"I'm here for you" or
"I don't want to leave you."

When Dad died, many people said they would be there, that they would always be there. They did offer to talk, but as I mentioned in the early stages, I didn't trust anybody, I didn't feel able to talk. Over time, they stopped asking probably because they believed I didn't want to.

74

Eventually they stopped asking.

This is where it gets confusing, even as a child so young I think this was self-protection, a way to gauge if they were trustworthy, could I let them in despite the fear of being left again?

This is what I mean when I talk about gentle consistency, even weekly or monthly, just a check-in.

"Are you okay?"

"Do you feel ready to talk?"

"Would you like to talk about the person and how you feel/felt?"

When people stopped asking, self-protection told me, I had been correct in not trusting those adults.

Did they care? How could they? They stopped asking if I wanted to talk.

Over the months, one by one the adults who had made that promise to always be there, slowly moved on with their own lives, their own families. They stopped visiting, they stopped checking in on us or seeing us. This once big family had all dispersed into, I'm sure, their own world of guilt and grief.

The abandonment felt real all over again, from those who were left behind, those who had said they would always be there for us. I say this not through wishing to cause those adults guilt, I have forgiven them and discuss this later in the healing process. I highlight this with the intention to raise the importance of keeping your word.

Please consider what you are offering in making this promise to a child, it is highly likely they have lost trust in adults, you will/can be part of helping them to regain trust.
It's okay to say,
"You know where I am if you need me" but also take the lead, be the adult, check in regularly as well as offering to be there when needed.

Actions speak louder than words.

So begins a lifetime of finding it nigh on impossible to trust people.

Some of the issue was Mum did find a new partner. She moved on with her life. That was her as an adult. It was not us as children, or our decision, we were still the same children who needed our extended family. That didn't change. If anything, that made us need Dad's family even more, the part of our life from when he was here. However difficult it is for adults to see the wife/husband/partner move on after the death of the loved one, that should not change the relationships and bonds with the children left behind. That is for adults to navigate, because as a child we are searching for connection and support.

I know this isn't easy, I know this must be incredibly difficult for adults. Meeting the children's needs can remain priority at the hearts of all adults.

This may sound selfish, everything all about the child, not how it works in the real world? This is my inner child's insight. Any child who loses a parent to suicide is just that…. an innocent child who didn't ask or expect this to happen. We do need extra support, love and validation. To feel we matter. We are valued and wanted. That includes feeling that adults are working together to provide this reassurance.

*Maybe I look like a happy child playing in the garden. Maybe I look like a child coping and playing in the place I love most… outdoors. Freedom in being alone and just being me. Playing out in the garden feels like a little imaginary world where I can pretend.*

*Maybe I look like a child playing with her dog. Having a companion.*

*This might be what the adults see when I catch a glimpse of them checking on me out of the window. They give a little wave back, maybe they think I am a happy child at play. Maybe they think I have forgotten what happened, maybe they think I am okay. Maybe they are worried about me, but don't know what to say to me. I know they still have their grown-up conversations about Dad while I'm out in the garden playing.*

*The truth is, I am not okay. I am lost and I am lonely. I am just a little girl with a heart that's been broken, and I don't know how to fix it. I don't know ways of collecting all these broken pieces and put them back together. It's just me and these thoughts, my own voice trying to talk to me about the world and the meaning of life.*
*"Why are we here on earth?"*
*"Does it have to be so deep?"*
*"Why does it feel like big thoughts all the time?"*

*"Why can't my mind just think of playing with dolls and having fun?"*

*The little girl they watch out at play is busy trying to right the wrongs of what happened.*

*There are no words to describe the friendship and bond I have with my dog, Delilah. She is a Golden Labrador; she was Dad's dog. She is always by my side. Willing to listen to my questions and thoughts that spin round my head. When we cuddle, I feel a kind of magic between us, she helps the pain go away, just a little bit. It's like she can feel my hurt and is my friend. I find it easy to talk to her, I don't have to feel worried about what she might think, she will not tell me to try and get over it. I feel comfortable to talk with her, it helps that some of my thoughts are out of my head and shared with her.*

*I love the dandelions in the garden, they are so fascinating. A perfect circle just waiting to be blown as you watch the fluffy seeds dance off in the wind. Something Delilah and I have fun doing together. She makes me giggle as she tries to sniff them, they get stuck to her little wet nose.*

*What are children encouraged to do with a dandelion when they blow it?*

*Make a wish.*

*The wishes for me are always the same:*

*"I wish you hadn't left."*

*"I wish I could wake up and this all be a bad dream."*

*"I wish you didn't feel that the only way to leave was to take your own life."*

*"I wish I could start this thing called life again and this pain not to be part of it."*

*I know that these wishes cannot come true.*
*I am wishing for things that can never happen.*
*I'm a child, I use my wishes in hope, if I wish hard enough,*
*somehow maybe this will all go away. Like in the films where the*
*happy ever after happens.*

*Being able to disappear into fantasy play, I often make up*
*scenarios in my head, where you haven't died. Maybe the grown-*
*ups have lied, you have just moved somewhere far away. That one*
*day you will return, pick me up in your arms give me a great big*
*cuddle and things will be better again. I would be upset they lied,*
*but it gives hope that you can return. I will see you again, there is*
*an explanation to why you left, and they told me you had died.*

*This must be part of my brain that wants to heal the hurt, because*
*when I pretend this, I don't have to be in the present and it isn't*
*real. When I let myself feel that it isn't real, and you are*
*somewhere else this doesn't hurt. I know this is just a game I can*
*play, a trick on my mind, because when it's time to stop playing in*
*the garden and return to the house, you are not there. Seeing the*
*grown-ups upset brings me back to the reality that it is indeed true.*

*If you get the chance to fantasise about a situation, do you ever*
*allow the thoughts of normality to play a part? Do you picture hurt*
*and loneliness?*
*Pain and abandonment?*

*I didn't.*

*To look from the outside, you don't know I'm in my own little world. You don't know its where I escape this emptiness.*

# Help me feel seen

*I've been having some emotional outbursts lately. I don't know where they come from. Sometimes it can be a comment or a rush of anger and frustration. It happens when I feel invisible in the house. I'm dysregulated I throw things and hit the floor with my fists. Sometimes the pain is so bad that screaming and shouting helps for a moment. The tears don't always come, so maybe you think I'm not sad. You walk away from me, I cannot contain the rage, am I that unimportant to you? Do you not care that I am this upset?*

*I don't want to need you, I don't want to take up your time, I don't want to be uncontrollable like this. I want to hurt myself. I want this pain to be real, a physical pain I can feel. I don't like me or these feelings, I want to punish myself.*

*I'm ashamed to tell you this, I don't want my friends and family to know this is how I act at home.*

*You feel safe Mum, to let these emotions out, I can only do this with you. I say things I don't mean, to shock you, keep you engaged in this conversation. I love you. I need you. Help me with these emotions I can't control. Stay with me. Please don't walk away.*

*Laying on the bed, my outburst now calming, I stare into space. Tears falling down my cheeks I know it would end like this. It always does, I lose control, and you go downstairs, I lay on the bed longing for you to come check on how I am. Sometimes I put Freddie songs on, think about the days that have gone. I wait for you to come and see me, hug me and tell me you understand. That even though I lose my temper, you still love me. I don't feel wanted or important ever since your partner moved in.*

*I can hear you watching TV with him, chatting and having a nice evening. Why am I not enough to come and help?*

*The thing is, I don't know how to express my feelings. I'm not even sure how to name all the things I feel.*

*The big ones are easier to show or tell you about. Sad or angry, frustration and happy I can name.*

*It's the ones I can't name, the ones that confuse me and make me feel new things, these are the ones that I struggle with.*

*Maybe I am jealous of your new partner, jealous he gets your care and attention. I don't know how to express this, so it manifests as an outburst.*

*All I crave is you to come and sit with me. Let me and my emotions be seen and be valid. I don't need you to talk. I don't need you to try and fix me. I just need you to sit in this room, while I cry, while I stare into space. Come and sit with me, so I know I'm not alone. Sit with me, understand my confusion is as real as yours. Sit with me and cry too, let me into your hurt, let me comfort you. Sit with me and listen to Freddie songs. Sit with me and talk about the happy memories. Sit with me and just talk about him and how much you miss him too.*

*Sit with me in silence, we can look at photos and not speak if it is too painful. Let us just look at them, remind me he isn't forgotten. Tell me you loved him. Speak about him with a smile, it's okay for us to smile about him. Just be with me, just me and you. No siblings, no partner or other family members. Just us, that would let me feel seen. Just some of your undivided attention. Once I'm calm, come lay with me, rest your head on me and let me know it's okay.*

*Lay with me and fall asleep next to me, its scary sleeping alone with these feelings. Don't just tell me that I am important, show me. Be here with me. Show me you are vulnerable too. Help me to build my worth, let me know you think I am worthy of love and care. Tell me why it's important to have self-love and self-care.*

*It does not have to be hours, just check on me after an outburst. Come back consistently so I know you are thinking of me, like I am you. Help me work my way through this confusion. Let discuss emotions, why they are intense and change so fast.*

*The nights I love the most, when you think I'm asleep and come kiss me on the head. Whispering I love you.*

*Even if we haven't talked about the meltdown, I love it when you kiss me goodnight.*

*I know this is all hard for you too. I know you hurt. I know you can't manage my behaviour; I need you to know I wouldn't choose to do this, it's out of my control.*

# *Help me feel seen – a poem*

A young girl, just eleven,
I am told: "Dad's gone to Heaven"

Lonely and lost,
Heartbreak isn't the only cost.

Tears within eyes, they sparkle and glisten,
I just long for ears that can listen.

Being told this pain will ease,
Screaming inside, "Just hold me please"

Let's talk of days that have already been,
I need you to help me feel seen.

The confusion I feel,
Know that it's real.
Childhood feels over,
Somehow, I'm much older.

I'm still a child the adults see,
However, I'm learning a new way to be me.

Sometimes I shout out,
But I love you, have no doubt.
Searching to find some self-worth,
What is my purpose on this earth?

This overwhelm is a trial,
Please come sit for a while.

I may have moments of play,
It doesn't mean that I'm okay.

I want you to remember,
I am grieving too,
Come hold me tight,
Model it will be all right.

I need you to guide me,
Set these emotions free.
Not to lock them up inside
Where no-one can see.

## Education, school and friendships

There has long been a fixation on the importance of education and schooling for children. Back in the 1990s, school was an important part of education for children, there didn't seem to be the pressure there is in the education system now. There still is little appreciation for life education and the skills we gain that simply cannot be taught. Achievements are recognised for those who can take in information, retain it and do well in exams. School isn't the only place education takes place; I feel that there is little credit for emotional intelligence. School for me wasn't about education or learning. No-one seemed to take in to account I was grieving and surviving a traumatic life experience. It was back to school as normal; I was expected to continue as my peers were. I realise now how unrealistic that was. You can't place a child back into school and expect them to learn in the way they did before.

*Mum decides not to return to the family home. She still finds it too hard to go back to the house without Dad. We can't stay at my Aunt and Uncles forever, we are now staying in a family member's mobile home on their land in the village. The positive to this is I don't have to return to the school with that horrible girl that bullied me. It means I can return to the village school. Back with friends that I know and have grown up with. Mum says she thinks it will be good for me to go back to school and gives me a card from friends. There are messages from friends, they are sorry to hear about Dad, they are looking forward to me going back to school. It feels nice that they have thought about me and care enough to send a card. I don't want to seem ungrateful, so I smile at Mum, say thank you. What I'm feeling deep inside is completely different.*

*This confirms my fears, they all know. Everyone knows Dad has died.*

*"Have they been talking about him, like the men in the shop?"*
*"What do they know about him?"*
*"Do they know he took his own life, or do they simply know he died?"*

*It's that powerless, no control of the situation that makes me feel unsafe. Maybe I don't want everyone at school to know. Maybe I don't want them to all be talking about it. No-one has asked me; no-one thinks to ask if I want to tell people in my own time. Or maybe I don't want anyone to know. The gossip in the shop made the outside world feel unsafe, now I have that feeling about returning to school. To others it's just something that has happened, it doesn't affect their lives, but to me, this is my life. My whole life, my world been turned upside down and I'm not sure how to cope with it all. Nothing I can do to change it now, but I'm aware the first time I walk back into school.*

*Everyone knows.*

*Walking back into the playground, everything is familiar, the building, teachers, and children. Yet everything feels so different now. I'm here, well, physically here, but it doesn't feel real. It's like my mind isn't here. My mind continues to feel like I'm not really in this world, like my body moves and does things, the things I'm meant to be doing. I just don't belong. I allow myself to glance over to the cemetery. I can see Dad's grave. I know he is there now and it's a constant reminder.*
*I don't think any adult has even considered that it is literally in my face as a reminder.*

*Some friends welcome me back and say it's good to see me. That's a nice thing to hear and it feels good to be surrounded by friends again. There is an awkwardness though, it's not the same as when I left. Some say they are sorry to hear that Dad has died. I don't really know what to say. Just the thought of him and what happened makes me sad, but I appreciate that some are brave enough to mention it. Others are just looking at me, maybe even having their own conversations about it. Some don't talk to me, maybe because they don't know what to say and that's okay with me. I know this is going to take a long time to adjust to and I can't be sure if these thoughts are real.*

*"Are they really talking about me?"*
*"Or is my mind just telling me they are?"*

*One boy from a few years below confirms my inner thoughts. Standing in the line for lunch he casually asks, "You're the girl whose Dad died, aren't you?"*

*It catches me off guard and everyone starts to look at me.*

*It's very overwhelming and far too much attention on me. Some others tell him not to ask me things like that and leave me alone. They are trying to look after me, I guess.*

*"Erm, yeah" is all I can manage to respond. My body has gone shaky again, I feel I might start to cry, and I don't want to. I don't want to cry and make a fuss. I don't want everyone to be looking at me. I don't want this to be happening. I don't want to feel this different to everyone else.*

*Someone must of told my older cousin, later, at lunch break, he appears in the playground.*

*He pulls the boy to one side and tells him sternly, "Leave her alone and don't ever mention to it to her again… Understand?"*

*The boy nods his head.*

*"It's okay, he was just asking a question." I say.*

*It wasn't this boy's fault; he was saying what others must be thinking. It was an innocent question. I don't feel like he said it to be mean or upset me. I know it's come from a good place. I know my cousin wants to protect me from the pain and people talking, but it feels like he has added to the awkwardness, now others will be worried about upsetting me through fear they will get in trouble. And all the while, no adult or teacher has any input. No-one is here to guide us through this strange situation we find ourselves trying to navigate.*

*So, this is school life and friendships for me now, and the feeling of isolation begins. I don't know if it will ever leave me.*

*Sometimes at play time, I see Nan at the grave, weeding and placing flowers down. I run over and say hello, it comforting to see her familiar face. What I really want is to be with her, for her to take me with her. I must be at school; that's what the adults tell me anyway. They don't really listen or understand that I don't feel like I fit in here. I can't shake this feeling off that I don't fit in anywhere. I notice my brain doesn't concentrate on lessons, like it does for others in the classroom. In geography, when the teacher talks about clouds, different shapes and names for them, I'm looking at the sky wondering if there is a Heaven.*
*"Do people who die really go there?"*
*"Do they live happily in the clouds?"*

*"What do they do all day, can they see the other people who have died?"*

*"Why did Dad want to go there and not be here in the real world"*

*Before I know it, the lesson is over, I've not taken in any information or learned what the cloud shapes are called, I can't say I really care.*

*Maths lessons are similar, others are going through the times tables and reeling off numbers in some pattern; I don't understand it. I don't want to understand it. My mind seems foggy, my head still spins from what is happening within my thoughts. Not having an interest in learning any of these things, what's the point? What is the point in anything? We all die anyway so why do we need this information. I have no space left for numbers and cloud names.*

*Being told school is an important part of childhood doesn't make any sense, the only thing that seems important to me is trying to work out why these things have happened and why my childhood seems so much harder than it is for the other children in my class. School isn't about learning for me, rather somewhere that I don't have a choice about going. As time goes on it starts to feel 'normal-ish' again, whatever normal is now. I still haven't figured out what that is. I have friends and get on with other children, but I never get a sense of belonging. I have this strange niggle in the back of my mind that they will leave me one day, that people are not here forever. I can't handle that feeling of being rejected by others, so maybe part of the issue with having close friends is that I don't allow myself to get close. I don't make strong connections like other friends do. They develop a trust for each other, I don't trust anyone now. It's not a pleasant feeling, but I figure that if I don't get too close to friends, I can't get hurt by them when they move onto other friendships. This happens a lot from what I observe; one day groups of girls are claiming to be best friends and all close, the next they are falling out over little silly things. The only way I can explain this is to say, I'm just here, almost observing school life, but not fitting in or finding my place.*

*Unfortunately, for me anyway, Mum decides it's time to move back to the family home, which was difficult to adjust to. Not only because we return to the house we lived in with Dad, but it means I must return to the middle school in town. As if life hasn't been confusing and unsettling enough, now it means leaving the friends I know in school and returning to the school I never settled in.*

*The only good thing I can say is the girl who bullied me relentlessly for taking her friends away has moved to a different school. I had not made any close friends when I was here before, so going back is super isolating. I think they must know that Dad has died, but this isn't mentioned and, in many ways, I'm grateful. I don't want to be here or to learn. There is a new situation going on now as well. Mum has a new partner; I don't get along with him; I hate being at home. So, although I am lonely at school and don't like it, it's better than the atmosphere at home. It isn't for too long though, as it's time for us to all move to upper school.*

*Daunting.*
*There is no other way to explain how I feel about this. Sure, many friends feel this too, we are told this is a natural feeling when moving on to a bigger school. It runs deeper than this for me. It's the idea of all the new people, situations and conversations I will have to have again. Three middle schools feed into the upper school, so there will be my friends again from the village, and this brings some comfort for sure. There is also a different middle school in town, which means lots of new people to meet. It isn't starting a bigger school that is troubling me, it's all the new friendships, which means the awkward conversations, which will, without a doubt, arise as we are encouraged to get to know each other.*

*I would like the world to swallow me up and not have to face any of this.*

*There is a shift in hormones, emotions and typical teenage life to work out, but with an added confusion about how I feel about life, friendships and education. I still can't get my head around the importance of school and what it is teaching us in terms of real life. It's been a few years since Dad has passed, but this unfamiliar environment and meeting lots of new people has really brought back memories and feelings. I start to consider things from an older perspective: What life would have been like if Dad had stayed?*

*"Would I be enjoying school life?"*
*"Would friendships be easier?"*
*"Would I feel less different?"*

*I don't know the answers, so all I can do is carry on as best I can.*

*One horrible day in a religious education (RE) lesson the topic is suicide.*

*It's an average school day. This afternoon we have RE, we gather in the classroom and take our seats. The teacher starts speaking, "Today we will be discussing suicide."*

*My heart leaps into my mouth and my stomach churns like it would on a rollercoaster ride. This topic has taken me by complete surprise, I feel sick. In fact, I'm not sure that I won't vomit. As she starts talking more, I can't hear her, my heart is pounding so fast I can hear it in my ears. I have the underwater feeling rush over me and the feeling of wanting to run and hide. I can't cope like this for an hour. My head begins to feel funny, like in a film, I can feel the others that know about Dad and my past staring at me. I'm sure I can feel them talking to each other, maybe gossiping to the ones that don't know telling them. Anger is bubbling inside, wanting to shout out to the teacher to shut up.*

*"Why are they talking about this?"*
*"Why is there no warning" just boom… straight into the subject.*

*I hear her say that it was considered a sin, a crime many years ago.*

*"What?? What are you talking about?" I think to myself.*
*"They had committed a crime by committing suicide."*

*I shudder, the meaning behind the phrase, committing suicide, is starting to fall into place.*

*"Is this what people thought/think?"*

*"It isn't a crime. It's someone suffering and hurting so badly that they take their own life."*

*She continues,*

*"They believed that they wouldn't go to Heaven, rather to Hell for their crime."*

*"Who the Hell does she think she is talking about?"*
*"Who gets to judge someone in that way and make such hurtful statements."*

*My hope, my comfort, is that my Dad had gone to be in a better place. I'm not sure I believe in a Heaven, but a happy after life where one day I will see him again. Be reunited. That's the only thing that has ever given me peace and hope.*

*To hear this utter rubbish pushes me over the edge. I can't hold it in any longer. I'm shaking and furious.*

*I push my table over in rage, shout at her that she doesn't know what she is talking about and run out of the door.*

*Standing in the corridor outside the huge tears roll down my face and I can't hold it in, sobs of despair pour out.*

*I'm waiting to get told off, sent to the head teachers office even. I don't care, I will tell them how wrong that teacher had been in what she was saying. I want to run, run far away and hide. If home was a happy place, I would run home. But there is no understanding there, I would probably get in more trouble because they don't listen.*

*The teacher, an older lady that I usually like, comes slowly out of the door.*

*"I am so sorry. Your friend has just told me about your Dad, I didn't know. For what it's worth, I don't believe that he will not have gone to Heaven. This is the curriculum that we must teach."*

*"What?"*
*"Why would they need to teach this curriculum?*
*"What purpose does it serve?"*
*My mind is confused and thinking once more about how useless school is.*

*"I am sorry. Would you like to go to the toilet and get a tissue and take a friend?" she asks.*

*That's kind of her, I think. I know deep down she is a nice lady. But her kindness is making me cry more. I feel seen and that she understands how hard this must be.*

*I'm relieved not to be in trouble and apologise for pushing the table over.*

*The rest of the day is a blur, and the one thing I do know is, if anyone in my year group didn't know about my Dad, they do now.*

*My heart sinks.*

# Things to consider

- Is the child ready to return to school? Do they want to return to school?
- Conversations before they return to school and education.
    - Can the child verbalise or write down things that they are worried about?
    - Does the child have worries about telling their friends?
    - Would the child like someone else to inform friends/peers/teachers/school before their return?
    - Would the child like to be involved in those conversations?
    - Is there anything they feel is important for others to know?
    - Would they like to connect and talk to friends before they return to school?
    - Would they like a parent/adult to be present for the first conversations of sharing the news? For support in answering questions.
- Are there any adults at the school with whom the child feels comfortable, who could be their go-to/check-in person?
- Could the teachers be informed of the situation so that the child doesn't have to talk to different adults and explain?
- Could an adult be responsible to offer support and check-in at the end of each day/week/term, dependent on the stage of grief/time of return? For example, a daily check-in when they first return to school and then gradually extend to weekly/monthly check-ins as they settle back into school environment.

- Could the child identify a few close friends who would be supported by this adult to have some quiet sessions together, to explore feeling and develop knowledge on how to support and talk about the subject? To have guidance from an adult.
- Could the child be given a time-out card? For when they feel upset and overwhelmed. They may not be able to verbalise how they are feeling, but by showing a card are able to leave lessons/playground to access somewhere quiet, thus alerting an adult that they need some support and time out.
- Could the child have a gradual/part-time timetable to ease them back into school if they feel too overwhelmed to return full-time immediately?
- Are there any lessons/classes they particularly enjoy, e.g. art/music/drama, that they could initially return to, so school doesn't feel as demanding?
- Can the school arrange talking sessions/art therapy or counselling that can take place during school time, building this therapy into their daily/weekly timetable?
- Would the child rather that not everybody knows?
- When moving to a new school/upper school for the school to be aware of the child's loss to suicide.
- For staff teaching any subjects about suicide, to know the child's situation.
- School to discuss with parents that it is a topic and for consent for the child to attend that lesson. Does the child want to attend that session?
- Give notice/warning before jumping into that topic in a lesson.
- If it is a topic that must be taught, offer extra support and be mindful about the terminology used.

- When moving to upper/secondary school, offer the time-out card and a quiet space, even if the child has been grieving for years the overwhelm and new friendships may need extra support.

# Visiting the grave

Some of the advice I have been given or overheard throughout the years…

"Have you tried going to the grave and talking to him?"

"Let him know how you feel, vent your anger, talk about the sadness you feel."

"Tell him that you miss him."

"Talk to him about what's going on in your life."

The problem with this is no-one explained what talking therapy was. That, yes, eventually over time it would help to process and accept the fate of what had happen in childhood. No-one explained that this takes time. Maybe they assumed I somehow just knew, but I didn't. How could I?

My ideal was for the pain to stop, the healing people talked of to begin. No-one explained what that would look like, no-one guided me through that. In fact, anytime his name was mentioned or brought up, the pain others must have still felt lead to a change in topic and shut down. Naïvely I thought that the adults had healed. This I now know is not true and many of them bottled it up because it was too painful to talk about.

Holding that pain in, not sharing brings a lifetime of the burden of grief. Sharing the pain, letting it out and connecting with others could have hopefully brought a stronger connection within the family rather than watch as it isolated people in their own grief.

~

*"Why would I want to visit the grave?"*

*"Why would I want to come and talk to you when you abandoned me?"*

*"You choose to leave, how can coming to talk to you even make anything better?"*

*"I don't want to visit you…talk to you…why should I?"*

*"Anyway, how the Hell is that going to help?" I think angrily to myself.*

*"It is not going to bring you back or change what happened."*

*"Bloody stupid idea if you ask me."*

*"Nope, I would rather not, thanks."*

*Now I am 15-years-old and struggling massively with my mental health. The thoughts that had started when I was 11 after you passed away have continued to play heavy on my mind. I don't remember too much of it for the first few years, I blocked you out of my mind. I don't want to think about you or what you did. That only worked for so long and it has taken its toll.*

*I decide I will visit your grave.*

*Sitting on the grass at the edge of your grave, just as Mum did the day of the funeral, I am not that little girl now. You are going to get teenage me now, full of attitude and frustration.*

*I am telling you straight, no holding back, no love involved.*

*"I am so angry and p\*\*\*\*\* off with you."*

*"Why did you do it? Why were we not enough?"*

*It is a different stage of life. I am not just a child now. The little girl who loved and admired you.*

*This is no longer the case, home life is vile, I have no way to escape it. It is where I must live, it's one of the most hostile miserable environments anyone could ever wish to imagine.*

*I am not naïve, I know no one could replace you. They couldn't, even if they were amazing. They wouldn't be you. Mum met a new man; I don't like the feeling I get in his presence. There is just something I can't put my finger on, but he makes me uncomfortable. He lives in our house, your house. I can't do anything about it, that powerless feeling arrived again. Out of my control, feeling unseen and unheard. No-one seems to care how this situation makes me feel, how I feel you are being replaced too soon. I was just a child then, my views not taken into consideration. It felt far too soon for someone else to be living with us. Mum knows how I feel, but everyone thinks I'm being difficult for no reason.*

*I hear things like this from everyone.*

*"Oh sweetheart, you will get used to him in time."*

*"It's going to be hard seeing Mum with a new man."*

*Nope, this isn't the case. It's not that I don't want Mum to be happy, or to move on, it's just something about him. No-one will listen to me; no-one is hearing what I'm saying. I'm just stuck in this unhappy home.*

*He seems emotionless and my instinct is always that he doesn't want to be around us three girls. He isn't kind, fun, or loving in anyway. All he wants is to be with Mum*
*and for us to be out of the way.*

*The other adults can't see that though, they don't live behind our closed doors.*

*He sends a shiver down my spine with one look when he is in one of those moods. It's like he has some strange control over Mum and has put a huge barrier between us. I don't want to act the way I do towards her, I shout, call her names. It makes no difference. She always chooses him. I have physically lost you, Dad, as a parent, but I very quickly feel I have emotionally lost Mum as a parent too.*

*Mums new partner, for the purposes of the book, will only be referenced as He/Him.*

*He does not like me because I have a voice and fight in my belly.*

*Charley and Izzy do not. They are younger and don't fight back.*

*That's the thing, if He was a kind-hearted man, He could be raising them with love and care, they could have some kind of father figure…….it is clear to me that was never in his plans.*

*He moved in just 9 months after you died, I took a dislike to him the moment I met him. He is cold towards us. He makes it clear we are not his children and doesn't want us to call him Dad.*

*Well, that is fine by me, because he does not deserve that title.*

*I could understand it with me, I was just turning 12 years old when he moved in, I was angry at the world, vocal in my thoughts and did everything in my power to get Mum to leave him. I felt isolated, alone, and empty.*

*I need you to understand it was not just because he wasn't you, Dad. It was because of his personality and the way he treated us all.*

*It's not a case of… "Most kids don't like their parent's new partner…"*

*I have been invalidated repeatedly with this old chestnut of a saying for a long time.*

*I feel daft talking out loud to you, but I'm so frustrated I don't care if someone overhears me.*

*"If you had stayed, things would not be this hard at home. He would not be in our lives."*

*"You should be here to protect me and my sisters, your daughters."*

*There I have said it. My truth… My thoughts.*

*"Is that what you want? Is that what you want to hear? Is that what everyone wants me to do?"*
*Talk to you, tell you how I feel.*
*"Is this meant to make me feel better?"*

*Four years, I have not spoken to you, four years I have not told you my truth… now I have.*

*I sit for a moment, I wait…. and I wait some more.*

*"Come on then, where is this magical wave of relief?"*

*"I've talked to you, I've told you my feelings, when is the pain going to stop?"*

*"When is this unbearable aching feeling in my heart going to stop?"*

*"Talking to you will make it easier, that's what they told me."*

*"I am here in desperation now, make this feeling to go away."*

*I sit here the whole sunny afternoon… waiting to feel differently.*

*I can't help but feel they lied to me.*

*This hasn't made it feel better.*

*I am 15-years-old, I've never had help with this, never talked to anyone, so of course I have taken their words literally.*

*I walked out of the graveyard fuming. I've wasted my afternoon waiting for something to happen. For the pain to ease. I guess it was a first step though.*

*I can't say I feel nothing, but equally, I can't say I feel something either.*

*Half laughing to myself,*

*"What do they know about this healing stuff?"*
*I'm tired, exhausted of carrying this pain.*

*Fully aware I have a whole lifetime ahead of me.*

*\*\*\*\*\*\*\*\*\*\*\*\*\*\*\*\*\*\*\*\*\**

*I'm 16-years-old now and I find myself drawn to your grave side once more.*

*This last year has been impossible.*

*The feelings just too overwhelming, just all too much.*

*I have come to you with a new emotion this time.*

*Empathy.*

*I nearly joined you a few months ago.*

*I genuinely wanted to, but for whatever reason, I wasn't successful.*

*I attempted to take my own life; I feel ready to talk to you about it.*

*"I've felt those dark thoughts now, realised that maybe it wasn't within your control."*

*"Maybe it wasn't something you had simply chosen to do."*

*"You were unwell too, right?"*

*In a strange way I feel connected and close to you, just like when I was a little girl.*

*"I understand you and you understand me. You understand what I'm saying, this brings me comfort, I can't talk to anybody else about this. This feeling of pure hopelessness and wanting to leave this world and be free of the pain."*

*I'm able to tell you how I truly feel and say, "Well, you just get it don't you?*

*For the first time sitting here at your grave I smile and even joke…*

*"Well of course you do, otherwise you wouldn't be buried in that box under the ground."*

*You listening to me in this moment, I don't feel so alone.*

*"This is strange, but I like it."*

*"Don't think it gets you off the hook though, I know in the moment of darkness how it feels to want to leave, how impossible it is to resist listening to that voice in your head."*

*"You know it's going to hurt the ones you leave behind."*

*I'm living proof of knowing how much that hurts, but even that wasn't enough to stop me trying to end it all.*

*"But I don't have children."*

*"Would I have been able to go through with it if I did? You must have been suffering so much not to stay for us."*

*"I will make a deal with you. I can't forgive you, but, I think, I understand it better now."*

*It is a strange feeling, knowing others who haven't experienced this won't be able to understand how it felt for you.*

*Promising I will be back another day, I walk away feeling different, not so angry or confused.*

*I still miss you, but it does not hurt as raw as it did in the beginning.*

*I don't keep my promise. It is years before I come and visit you again.*

*After my suicide attempt, the doctor says I was attention seeking. Yes, to a certain extent there is an element of truth to that statement, of course I need somebody to pay me attention, to listen and to help.*

*But, no, that was not my ultimate intention.*

*I wanted to be with you, I wanted the pain to stop, I wanted the tiredness to go away.*

*I tell the doctors, the professionals, Mum, I want to be successful, it isn't about attention…*

*I'm not sure they believe me.*

*They give me medication for depression, this will help they say.*

*I question how can popping a pill everyday possibly help? It won't change the situation, it won't change my life, or my experiences. I take them though, with hope the doctors know what they are talking about, however I don't have much trust in people these days.*

*Until my next visit to you*

*I'm 21-years-old now, I've just come out of a 5-year relationship, I feel lost and lonely again. Feelings of abandonment and rejection are flooding back.*
*"Am I not good enough?"*
*"Am I unlovable?"*
*"Why am I being left again?"*

*We grew apart, but losing someone that has been so close to me for five years feels unbearable.*
*"Why do people have to leave our lives?"*

*I'm not sure if these are normal feelings at the end of a relationship or if this is all heightened, as it unearths these deep childhood feelings. I had found a connection and loved someone, only for it to be gone again. When I speak to others, they don't seem to understand the intensity I feel about this relationship being over. They say we are just young, that love will be found again. I'm not sure I want to find it again, if it means we lose it.*
*I guess, that is the gamble of love and exposing our vulnerabilities to another.*

*I may be 21 and you have been gone for ten years, but the ache in my heart has not gone. I wish I could get one of your hugs now. You could make it better like you did when I was a little.*

*My ex and I got together a week after my attempt to take my life.*

*My mental health at its lowest, feeling unworthy of love and worthlessness. He sees the worth in me, something special in me that I couldn't. He helps save my life and turn the world from a loveless place and shows me I am loveable and important.*

*We had been friends at school, by some twist of fate, bumped into each other a few days after I left hospital.*

*He is a deep thinker and we speak about you. Something I have never done in this way before.*

*He understands how difficult my home life is. I am welcomed into his family. Given the chance of being part of what I can only imagine is what 'normal' family life is like.*

*It isn't perfect, I'm not daft. To me, however, it is very perfect. We sit round the table and have meals, talk about our day and there is never a cold atmosphere in their house. They even take me on holidays abroad with them.*

*Since my last visit to you, home life has deteriorated further. Mum got pregnant when I was 19.*

*I found this hard to accept and adjust to. Even at 19 years of age, I found it hard to see her start a family without you. It hurt to see her start a new family, especially with Him as He has always made it clear that we three girls are not his family.*

*Nobody in our house speaks for the first 6 months of her pregnancy. I wasn't home much; the atmosphere was impossible to live in.*

*Once our cute little sister is born, curly blonde hair and bright blue eyes, things seem to settle down. It was odd that He had never shown any fatherly interest in us, but is completely different with His own child.*

*He doesn't trust us with the baby. If she cries, he asks us, "What have we done to her?" If she vomits, he questions what have we given her? As though we have poisoned her. It hurts that he really thinks we would do something like that.*

*It becomes clear that He has his own mental health issues, that as a child/teenager I hadn't figured out. He is relentless, I develop anxiety about being around the baby. Maybe that was the plan, to make us uncomfortable to the point we just stop trying.*

*Nine months later, Mum tells us she is pregnant again.*

*This time my question is,*
*"How are we all going to fit in this house?"*

*I start my nursing diploma at university, but don't feel that the typical student life and dorms are right for me.*

*While Mum's in hospital having our baby brother, I move out.*

*It is a council flat and because of the size, they say two people must move in for the tenancy. My boyfriend and I decide to move in together. It is okay to start with, but it hasn't really been a choice. I feel rejected and the feelings from childhood creep back again, Mum putting Him first. I know I am an adult now with a life of my own, but I'm resentful, that house is Mum and Dad's house.*

*I must move out of the family house; I must take my boyfriend with me to get the flat. We didn't live together long, we grow up, we change, our lives are going in different directions. That's not to say it doesn't hurt though. With all the old feelings bottled up and never processing or healing my grief, I just don't know how to cope with these emotions.*

*********************

*This time I come to your grave it is dark, like middle of the night dark.*

*I've been to the pub in the village I don't know what time it is, but I think last orders have been called. I don't know what triggers in my mind, but I want to talk to you. I sneak out of the pub; even whilst drunk, I know someone will try and stop me. I stumble into the graveyard. I don't know how, but I find your grave. It must be like finding your way home after a night out, you don't really know how you get there, you don't remember, but somehow you arrive.*

*I know I'm drunk, because if I was sober, I would be pooping my pants. It's night, dark, and I'm in a cemetery alone.*

*I don't sit on the edge, as I usually do, I climb and sit on top of your grave.*

*I need to feel close to you and I don't want to leave.*

*Sobbing telling you this, I hear a familiar voice, "Madz… Madz…What are you doing darling? Are you okay?"*

*I snap back…*

*"What do you think? I'm sitting on a grave in the middle of the night."*

*I can't hold it in any longer.*
*"No, I'm really not okay, I just want this feeling to stop."*

115

*My friend has followed me, we have known each other since we were 5-years-old. Bless him, he is now trying to coax me away. "It is starting to rain," he informs me.*

*He knows my life, he has watched my life, I know he has always had a soft spot for me, he cares.*

*"Come on, let's go, you are getting wet," he suggests gently.*

*"You go, I will be okay, I just need to be here right now," I reply.*

*"Okay, but I'm staying with you," he says.*

*He sits next to me in the dark, in the rain, sharing this moment with me.*

*I don't know how long we stay here, with my stubbornness, not until I am ready to agree to leave. Walking back to his parents' house with his arm around me, "Come on Madz, you need to get some rest."*

*I don't know what would have happened to me that night, what state I would have been waking up the next morning, had my friend not been with me. Soaking wet and hungover sleeping on a grave. (I'm going to bet I wouldn't be the first person to have ever done that)*

*Unless you have felt grief that grips so hard, no-one should judge.*

*I will always be grateful for that friend, I'm not sure I've ever needed a friend to give me love and validation as much as I did that night.*

*I stopped drinking so heavily after that night, it didn't stop me drinking alcohol completely, but it highlighted I could not be doing the same every weekend.*

*********************

*I don't visit you for a long time after this.*

*I get into an unpleasant relationship and stupidly moved away. He pushes my mental health into real crisis and isolates me from everyone. He isn't a self-aware person. He love-bombed me at the start of the relationship, makes me feel incredibly special. Until he begins criticising my every move and action.  By this point I  feel trapped with no way to leave. Somehow, I find the strength to leave. He teaches me I will never get stuck in a relationship like this ever again. I have learnt a life lesson, that is his purpose in my life. I take my puppy dog, Roxy, with me. He isn't having her.*

*The first thing I do when I move back home:*

*Come to visit you to tell you all about it.*

*I'm 25-years-old now and I'm free. I'm growing and learning life lessons, navigating my way through relationships. No-one will ever treat me like that again, Dad. If you were here, I'm sure you would have punched his lights out.*

*I will never need a man in my life, I would like to want one, but I will not depend on one.*
*For some reason, a quote from grease the movie pops into my head.*

*Frenchy saying,*

*"The only man a girl can depend on is her Daddy."*

*"Well… you ballsed that one up, didn't you Dad?" I say out loud, giggling.*

*I sarcastically give you a thumbs up… "Cheers!"*

*I think you may have understood my sense of humour... even if you don't, you can't answer me back.*

*For the first time ever and something I never pictured myself doing, I leave the cemetery giggling, with a vastly different feeling to any I've ever had before.*

*I've got my own little flat with my chocolate cocker spaniel, Roxy. She is only a few months old and, my goodness, I love her like no animal I've ever loved before. I tell her everything, I talk to her for hours, she is always obliging to lick away my tears. "Urgh," I hear some of you say, "that's disgusting."*

*It is comforting, she is my best friend. The perfect companion I need more than I realised. It reminds me of the bond I had as a child with Delilah. I hadn't expected that level of comfort to be even greater as an adult with a dog companion.*

*Back in my hometown now, Mum's house is only a minute walk away, I love being back close to home, but not having to enter that house. I have a happy little space of my own now.*

*When I am 24-years-old, Mum has her third child with Him, another baby boy. Don't get me wrong, it feels strange at 24 seeing Mum having a baby, friends of my own are parents now.*

*When she tells me she is pregnant this time, I don't live at home. Although "I can't say I am thrilled about it" I'm able to think, "Whatever. It's up to you what you do."*

*Charley has a boyfriend with a family she feels loved and wanted by. She moves in with his family. I am so happy for her.*

*Izzy has a boyfriend she seems happy too. Spending her time with his family.*

*I'm pleased we find these happy houses and families.*

*Izzy and I started to bond as adults now, we have missed a fair few years, I work as a nurse in an old people's home and my shift patterns are all over the place. I try to visit home; I hate the fact I must leave my sisters in that house. It is hard to pull the strength together to go back there to that atmosphere to visit.*

*You just never know what mood will greet you. When it's good, we talk, laugh, drink wine and have dinner. Other times you can pop round, say hi, and get the glare and silence. He will disappear upstairs.*
*"What's up his arse now?" I'd ask Mum.*
*Always just a shrug, 'Oh I don't bloody know, He's been in this mood for… (sometimes days and sometimes weeks)."*

*It has been this way forever, so it's quite normal. We do have good times, as the three young children grow up, we have days out, trips to the zoo, we do have some form of family life… it just only happens when He decides to engage and wants to do these things with us.*

*It doesn't change, even when we are grown up, one of us is always in His bad books, getting the silent treatment. While the other two get the conversations and chats. It is just potluck as to when it becomes your turn.*

*It had been consistent through childhood; it is our normal. We all notice this isn't something we experience at other's houses.*

*That said, you wouldn't be aware or know if you visit our house. He can be like this with visitors too, but never on the level we experience it. It's weird, the way he chats to us and joins the conversation, but when visitors leave, back to the glare and silence. Our boyfriends witness it, experience it first hand for themselves. They too, enter our house and are welcomed or are given the glare as he walks out the room.*

*Eventually it comes to the point they mouth… "rude", as he leaves the room. Love them, it doesn't stop them coming to our house. There is something very comforting, them seeing/feeling these behaviours. We have people who see what our home life is like. We aren't over dramatic, we don't get on with him, they feel that themselves.*

*I hate Izzy being left at home. I don't want her to move in with her boyfriend so young, just to escape like Charley and I have.*

*I can do for her, what I longed for someone to do for me, and save her from that house.*
*"Move in with me and Roxy?" I suggest*
*I don't have much, it's a crappy two-bedroom flat with not much in it. I've just left my ex and left pretty much everything with him. I don't care, I have a safe space,*
*"Come and share it with me?"*

*I don't have to ask Izzy twice, in a heartbeat she moves in. We are free. We love it. Life is good.*

*It doesn't stop us from feeling incredibly guilty and sad leaving Mum. At the end of the day, it has been her choice. They have a family of their own. We can't do anything about that... We are elated that we are old enough to leave.*

*********************

# Christmas 2007

*The first time I visit to wish you a Happy Christmas.*

*I don't like wreaths, don't ask me why, I just don't. I'm sure there is a meaning, I've never been interested enough to find out why. They don't scream Merry Christmas to me.*

*Maybe it's my inner child, but I start a tradition of my own. I bring a miniature Christmas tree and place it on the grave. There, that looks a bit more like Christmas, Dad.*

*Izzy lives with me now Dad, I'm happy, I think she is too. I don't need life to change, I want to stay like this.*

*I'm not looking for a relationship, to give me a connection. I don't need to be in a relationship to feel complete, I am happy being just me.*

*What a nice feeling, long may it continue.*

*The last month or so Izzy and I have been socialising together in the pubs in the village. It feels nice having her out with the bunch of regular pub goers, I've been coming for years and know most. Well, it is a small village everyone knows everyone! Izzy has even met a new boyfriend at the pub.*

*I'm telling you about how we had been out Christmas Eve together and how much fun we had. It was the busiest I've seen it for ages, lots of new faces.*

*There was quite a handsome new face that stood out, he has the most beautiful blue eyes, we shared a smile across the pub. I thought, "I'm going to try chatting with him later."*

*I'm a bit gutted Dad, I didn't get round to talking to him. The night just flew by, and the chance never came. At kicking out time, everyone is in the car park, smoking and singing "Merry Christmas." Izzy and I are waiting for a taxi home and her boyfriend waits with us.*

*I can tell this blue-eyed lad is younger than me, as he walks over and says, "Hi."*
*He informs me, "I've been wanting to talk to you all night."*

*"Oh, have you now?" I tease.*

*"Could I get a Merry Christmas kiss?' he asks, grinning.*

*"Go on then." I say, all giddy and daft.*

*From out of nowhere, he pushes me against the taxi and kisses me with some passion that I just wasn't expecting. I thought he meant a bit of a peck. Nevertheless, it's quite thrilling.*

*I hear a male voice shouting in the background… "Oi, what you are doing kissing Izzy's sister like that?"*

*He stops kissing me, whispers Merry Christmas in my ear, gives me a cheeky smile and wanders off.*

*"Merry Christmas indeed!" I smirk to myself.*

*The male voice is Izzy's boyfriend… "Madz, what are you doing kissing him like that?"*

*I reply, "I don't know, but it was fun. Do you know who he is?"*

*"Yeah, I do, that's my best mate... Leigh Roberts!"*

*That is that, around a week after the Christmas Eve kiss, Leigh and I swap numbers. I am in fact correct he is younger than me, just 21- years-old and laughing at me being an older woman, only by four years, but I'm not really thinking anything of this as a relationship.*

*Life is good now and no harm in having a bit of fun, I think, about time I let my hair down again. We arrange for him to come over with Izzy and her boyfriend, I am nervous, I was tipsy on Christmas Eve and not sure I completely remember what he looks like. He knocks on the door and greets me with a bottle of wine and 20 fags in one hand and a bag of Chinese food in the other… yep, I can see myself enjoying his company.*

*Those twinkly blue eyes are just as beautiful as I remembered, I whisper all giggly with Izzy in the kitchen as we dish up the food… "Oh, those eyes are just something else."*

*Leigh works away in the week and our weekends become about the four of us, take aways, drinking and nights out.*

*A few months later Leigh tells me he hasn't anywhere to stay. His Dad has moved to a one-bedroom flat; Leigh needs to find a place of his own.*

*"The offer is there if you want to stay here for a bit, nothing heavy, it isn't forever, just until you figure out what to do." I offer. Plus, he works away in the week so will mainly just be the weekends*

*Some idiot decides to rob the lead from the roof of our flat. I get a call from Izzy's boyfriend, "Madz, it's like it is raining inside the flat, I've got all the pots and pans out and catching as much rainwater as I can, but think you better come home."*

*The four of us must decide, are the boys going to go live together and me and Izzy find somewhere new? Or are we going to start our lives as couples in houses of our own?*

*It's likely going to end up with us living together as couples sooner or later, so let's give it a go.*

*\*\*\*\*\*\*\*\*\*\*\*\*\*\*\*\*\*\*\*\*\**

*The first year passes fast, I come to visit you more now Dad.*

*I'm in a good place, I bring Leigh to meet you, it feels right, I can't express the enormity of it all to Leigh, but he happily comes along while I place flowers down and joins me this first Christmas to give you the Christmas tree.*

*He doesn't look at me like I'm crazy while I talk out loud to you telling you what we have been doing.*

*A few months later, a very strange feeling takes over me… I come to tell you about this as I tend to the grave.*

*"I think I want a baby."*

*I did not see this coming… I have never wanted children, never wanted to give life to another soul who may feel the way I do.*

*Life hurts, life is hard, I don't want to bring someone else to that.*

126

*I do now, I love the idea of the love and purpose this can bring to our lives. Sure, people say parenting is hard and tiring, but it's usually followed by them saying how they wouldn't be without them.*

*Leigh is nervous about the idea, but broodiness is impossible to silence now I have it.*

*In the end he agrees, okay Mad, if this will make you happy, let's do it. What he or I didn't expect was me to be showing him a positive pregnancy test just a few weeks later. The shock must have got him good, as I hear him vomiting in the bathroom... Hang about, shouldn't that me being sick? I laugh at him.*

*********************

*I come to the grave, tell you I'm pregnant, I'm excited and happy, life seems to be… life, the pain of you not being here seems to have lessened, it isn't so intense.*

*********************

*I have a rough time in labour, pre-eclampsia means labour is induced and after a long day with no progression, an emergency C-section is needed.*

*On 1ˢᵗ January, a special way to start the year, Leigh and I become parents to a beautiful baby girl, Mikayla. I know whatever the future holds for us, I will love him always for giving me this baby to love.*

*This year, the snow is heavy and not being able to drive for 6 weeks while the c-section heals, I can't visit you.*

*************************

*I bring your very first granddaughter to meet you now the weather is better.*

*"I wish you could meet her; I find myself wishing you could be here once more."*

*I feel a wave of anger,*

*"Not only did you take away my Dad, but you also took the chance of my children having you as a Grandad."*

*I have a child of my own now, okay she may only be months old, but there is no force on earth that can take her away from me, I cannot leave her.*

*"How did you manage to leave us?"*
*"Was it that you didn't love us enough?"*
*"Or does this show me how unwell and desperate you were."*

*Mmmm, food for thought.*

*This feeling doesn't last long, I certainly don't have the time or energy to dwell on it.*
*Parenting is demanding work, I'm busy being a mum and it is exhausting. So, I briefly mention this to you and move past it. I learned back as a child; I can't change what happened and I certainly can't change it now.*

I must admit, I wasn't sure at times if Leigh and I would make it. Sleepless nights, pressure of money and adjusting to parenthood was no easy task. I found a new respect for Mum, well, all mothers really. This was a tough job…. I did joke with Mum… "Why on earth would you put yourself through this six times?"

She just giggled.

Mum was a doting Nannie. She popped in often, even if just for 10 minutes (she still had a young family to look after and worked full time, my youngest brother was still just 4 years old), but these pop-ins and knowing I can call her a million times at any time, night or day, help immensely.

*Somehow, we make our way through, it becomes easier, I guess we find our connection and adjust to family life.*

*Mikayla has not long turned 2-years-old, when that feeling creeps back……*
*"Leigh, can we have another baby?"*

*He rolls his eyes at me… "Oh no, here we go again!" he jokes.*

*Once more, the feeling is too strong, it's all I can think about (and go on at him about) Until, "Yeah okay Mad, if it makes you happy."*

*To our delight, it is only about a month or so later that I excitedly show Leigh a positive test.*

*This pregnancy flies by, I think having a toddler to keep me busy makes the time goes faster. Everyone is excited for the baby to arrive. We find out early on that we are having a boy.*

*Mum has tears in her eye, the kind of sad but happy expression when we inform her the baby's middle name will be Leon, in memory of Dad.*

*We seriously consider calling him Leon, but my fear is the sadness that will bring when family see him. The sadness and tragedy of Dads death. We don't want that for the baby or for myself every time I have to explain he is called Leon after my Dad. Then having to go through the sadness of the story each time.*

*Leigh and I agreed Leon as a middle name. It feels a perfect way to include Dad's name.*

*********************

*The most emotional visits to you.*

*I have another emergency C-section, but baby Harleigh and I are doing well. That is the important part.*

*I come to show you this beautiful baby boy, your first Grandson.*

*All I can do is sit and sob. It should be a happy visit, filled with joy.*

*Sobbing, through tears I tell you,*

*"Mum will be joining you soon."*

*There is nothing we can do. No way to prevent it from happening. Mum's been diagnosed with pancreatic cancer, she is only 47, there is no treatment that can save her.*

*"You will be there when her time comes Dad."*

*Back together. It is the only thing that brings me some comfort, but I don't want her to go. I don't want her to leave. I need her, I love her. We all need her here with us longer.*

## 22nd November 2013

Our wedding day.

Our wedding day is full of thoughts of you, Dad.
I can't visit the cemetery to show you my dress, but I am
thinking of you.

"You should be here to give me away."
"Walk me down the aisle, beaming proudly, giving a funny
speech about when I was your little girl."
I've been preparing for your presence to be missed on this
special day for years.
What I've not been prepared for is Mum being terminally ill.

Nine weeks ago, Leigh asked me to marry him. We know
Mum doesn't have much time left, her health is deteriorating
rapidly.
It isn't how I expected planning our wedding would be.
We have a ridiculously small budget, but that doesn't stop us.
The important thing is we are getting married. It brings us
together as a little family. I am excited to become Leigh's wife,
Mrs Roberts.
There is a pang of emotion, that I am unable to describe, that I
will be losing your family surname. No matter what my last
name is, I will always be your daughter.
If you can't be here to give me away Dad, in my heart it must
be Mum.
Mum is honoured when we asked her to give me away.

Weddings are emotional at the best of times, but today is an
extreme of emotions. Mum looks beautiful and is by my side.
She is frail now; my heart is breaking seeing her need a stick to
aid her to walk. Mum smiles all day; I feel her proudness/pride

glow through. We can only afford two hours with the photographer, she knows our situation and does an amazing job, capturing the happiness and joy. Beautiful memories that will last a lifetime, precious photos to keep forever. It is hard to keep the tears at bay, but everyone helps to make it special. A day we will never forget.

# 2017

Three years after Mum passed and broodiness creeps over me again.

It was not anyone's fault, but Harleigh babyhood, overshadowed by the sadness of Mum's illness. After her passing, life seemed a blur. I couldn't help but feel I needed to have one more baby. Leigh agreed and in October 2017 we welcomed our second baby boy, Vinnie. He completes our little Roberts family perfectly.

# *Things to consider*

- Explaining to the child/teenager the five stages of grief. Use age-appropriate language.

- The Kübler-Ross model[1] gives the five stages as
    - Denial
    - Anger
    - Bargaining
    - Depression
    - Acceptance

- Explore these emotions and feelings. They may or may not happen in this order. Let the child know they are normal natural stages of grief, and they may come and go.
  It may help with any confusion the child has around these emotions. It wasn't until I wrote this book and reflected, I could understand:

    - Child-me had made up fantasies in the early denial stage of grief
    - Teenage years had brought anger.
    - Depression in later teenage years

- With suicide, maybe we return to the anger stage at different life stages?
- Visiting the grave and talking to the person they have lost can bring comfort, can bring a sense that the person lost is still hearing about our lives and things that are happening. With an explanation this may or

---

[1] On Grief and Grieving: Finding the Meaning of Grief Through the Five Stages of Loss (Kübler-Ross, 2005)

may not help, it's individual and okay to want to do this or not.

With an understanding that this takes time to bring comfort and that on the first visit it won't bring healing.

# Alcohol and unhealthy coping mechanisms

*I'm about 17-years-old when I discover alcohol.*

*Friends have been drinking in the park for years, but it has not appealed to me.*

*At first it makes me feel strange, sick and dizzy, but it's fun, falling around and laughing at stupid things.*

*"Is this the type of carefree happiness others feel without a drink?"*

*"Is this what it feels like not to have to feel big emotions and worries?"*

*I don't talk about this to my friends, it is probably too deep of a conversation.*

*I don't think they would understand what I need to express, they haven't experienced loss to suicide.*

*Anyway, we are having fun and I'm forgetting all that.*

*I don't particularly like the taste, but then, at 18 years of age, I have ID. I can go into any shop and buy it freely. No-one can stop me, well who is there to stop me? No-one knows what I get up to in my free time.*

*The true danger is, not only is it easy to get a hold of, but I've learned it numbs this pain.*

*I don't have to think about anything when my brain feels fuzzy and numb. It helps for a while. Which is more than can be said for these tablets the doctor's given me.*

*Drinking quickly becomes my weekend activity of choice. It gives me the chance to be free of me.*

*I'm full of confidence and fun.*

*The life and soul of the party. It is great. For the first time since childhood, I'm loving life. Long may this continue I think to myself.*

*It helps keep me here in the world.*

*This continues for years. I'm doing other life things; I study health and social care for three years. I am a carer in an old people's home, I adore this job.*

*I find myself mothered by the older carers, I have company and connections with other adults. I have a purpose, I'm needed by the old folk, it's amazing to feel wanted and useful.*

*My friends question why from the age of 16 I want to be wiping old people's bums every day.*

*I realise, I've matured and grown up faster than most teenagers my age.*

*Working in the week and studying, drinking and socialising at weekends, I thought this is the answer to life.*

*The trouble with alcohol is it's easy to use alongside many emotions. Happy times and celebrations, have a drink. Sad and frustrated, have a drink. Socialising with others, feeling anxious, have a drink. Feeling alone and isolated, have a drink. It's hard to admit, but alcohol is my friend. Many times, I feel my only friend.*

*Non-judgmental, it does not care if I am having a good day or bad. It does not care if I ugly cry in distress and pain. It does not care if I sit in silence or if I am angry and throwing things in frustration. My companion that comes on all my experiences. Always there, always available, always obliging.*

*"Alcohol does not care, its incapable of love and care."*

*"It is easy to feel that alcohol cares as it can be a consistent companion".*

*"In truth, I ache for a friend, who can understand and just be with me. No judgment or telling me to what to do, or how to feel. Just someone to share the confusion".*

*The vulnerability and trust it takes to build these bonds with other people/friends is indescribable.*
*My trust for people is shattered, my self-worth is low. If a parent and family have not been able to offer the unconditional support and presence, how can I find that in a stranger?*
*I've been walked away from, misunderstood and left by some of my closest people. Plus, from others I have attempted to build friendships with.*
*I am too much for my own head and thoughts most of the time, why could/should someone else be able to understand that when I can't?*

*I struggle with my identity, who I am, what I enjoy. I've not built-up hobbies or interests, I've been trying to survive and make the thoughts in my head better.*

*Alcohol is a quick fix, it soon rushes to the brain and quietens the noise. The problem is over time it takes more to achieve this desired effect.*

*"I am ashamed that alcohol is my go-to comfort."*
*"People have views and opinions of those that use it."*
*"People judge it as a weakness."*
*Or have the idea you should*
*"Simply stop drinking it."*
*"It is not that easy when it feels like a medicine and comfort."*

*"Of course, the shame stops you from admitting what you do."*

*I never viewed myself as having an alcohol problem. Or that I abuse alcohol. The terms heard when people drink too much. I saw it as self-medicating, with something at the time helped.*

Recently I came across the work of Dr Gabor Maté, a Canadian physician with a special interest in childhood development and trauma.

Dr Maté believes that "The source of addiction is not to be found in genes, but in childhood trauma and in stress and social dislocation endemic to systems of inequality and injustice"[2].

According to Maté, "All addictions are attempts to soothe some kind of pain, often an emotional loss or trauma. Dealing

_____

[2] Hungry Ghosts (Dr Gabor Maté, 2018)
https://drgabormate.com/addiction/

with addiction, then, requires addressing (or 'being with') this pain. But in order to do that, addicted people need to be supported by and connected to, others."[3]

Reading Dr Gabor Maté's work gave me a much clearer understanding about how and why I've used alcohol. His approach to addiction by focusing on the trauma has been a turning point. Exploring my trauma and connecting to it has hopefully helped towards the recovery of not using alcohol to numb pain.

This really was a lightbulb moment; it was because of the lack of connection with others that I found a bond with alcohol. I hope that, moving forward, my connections with others will become stronger as I have been able to open up and share my struggles.

[3] The Opposite of Addiction Is Connection (SAND, 2015) https://scienceandnonduality.com/article/the-opposite-of-addiction-is-connection/

## *Things to consider*

- Being mindful of someone who has suffered trauma and if they are using substances to numb pain.
- The importance of connection and bond for teenagers/young people when facing a loss to suicide.
- Drinking may be a cry for help.
- Offering to support them in their grief and show them that they are not alone.
- Discuss how unhealed trauma may make them feel they need substances to numb pain but there are other healthier alternatives for them to cope.
- I would recommend looking at the trauma work/research of Dr Gabor Maté.

# My beautiful Mum

This, by, far is the hardest chapter to write.

It might come as a surprise, when the book is about losing a parent to suicide, it is the other parent that is the hardest to write about. There are deep wounds that need healing and processing for the relationship with the parent left behind. It was a huge responsibility for Mum to be left with three young daughters, while dealing with her own shock and grief after losing her husband; the person she had referred to as her best friend.

After 10 years, I haven't dealt with the loss of Mum. I've never felt ready. It felt like an impossible thing to heal from, subconsciously, I've always known that to grieve fully I need to make sense of our relationship from childhood.

Not from adulthood. Our relationship in adulthood was different, I loved her. Mum was my best friend and an incredible friend she was too.

To be able to heal from this loss, I focus on my inner child's wounds from the emotional neglect. That's hard to write, a horrible heavy hurt feeling, but to name the emotion, gives an opportunity to heal.

"My inner child felt neglected."
"That is something to validate."

Rather than saying Mum did her best. Which I know she did. Rather than saying Mum was an inspirationally strong woman. Which she was. Rather than trying to defend and protect her as a mum.

I need to allow my inner child to have her voice, to hold space for her to connect to the emotions and let them go too.

I write this with no judgment, no bad feeling, but to give insight into the impact and importance of connection and bond with the parent left behind.

Growing up, I always tried to remember Dad stories, early memories of Mum are not as strong. After Dad passed our mother/daughter relationship was strained.

I never blamed Mum in any way for his death.

What hurt to the core was Mum allowing her new partner to move into our home so fast. Dad's home, our family home. Uninterested in my thoughts or feelings about the situation. I do not want to dwell on the way things were, we both said things we didn't mean. As an adult I'm able to look at the situation through a different lens, Mum was 27-years-old, left by her husband in the cruellest of ways, with three young daughters and a mortgage. I honestly don't know how I would cope in that situation.

I understand now, Mum was angry at Dad, resented him for what he did to our lives. I never understood when I asked what she would do if you were to see him again and she replied, "hit him with a baseball bat."
How mean, I used to think, but I understand what she meant now.

Those years emotionally disconnected from Mum, when she got into her new relationship felt isolating.

After the attempt at taking my own life, it brought us the connection I'd always needed.

(Just to be clear, I am not implying this is the correct way to find connections with family. As I have previously stated, it wasn't my intention to gain attention, I didn't want to be here.)

Nevertheless, it brought attention to the fact I desperately needed help, my mental health at an all-time low. It must have been hard for Mum, the thought that she may also lose her daughter to suicide.

*I've been in sixth form today, I can't stop crying, I can't control the tears. I feel so hopeless, I can't hold in these feelings of despair.*
*I sit, head on the desk crying.*
*I no longer care if anyone sees me broken.*
*I feel broken and the truth is I have for a long time.*
*I get up to leave, a puddle tears left on the desk.*
*I do not know what to do, where to go, to whom to turn.*
*I cannot cope with this isolation.*
*The school ring Mum.*
*The home phone is ringing as I walk into the empty house. I do not refer to it as home, it doesn't feel like a home. Just a house where I live.*
*I answer it, it is Mum, telling me she loves me, she will be home as soon as possible. There is a panic in her voice, she tells me to hug the dog, talk to the dog, she knows Delilah is my companion.*

*"Just stay there Mad, I'm on my way."*

*I don't want to hug the dog; I don't want to wait for Mum to return.*

*"I wanted the pain to end…"*

*The front door bangs, oh no, I pray it's not my sisters.*

*"What have I done?"*

*Downstairs I see Him, Mum's partner, messing around in the mirror, asking if his top looked okay.*

*As he turned to look at me, immediately I see concern on his face.*

*"What's the matter with you?" he asks.*

*"I've done something, and I don't know what to do."*

*"I will call your Mum." he says in panic.*

*"Don't ring her, call an ambulance."*

*He gets in the ambulance with me, Mum will meet us in the hospital. Sitting in a cubicle, Mum arrives, she is sits one side and him the other.*

*The doctor tells us it's serious. Treatment is needed. I don't know how many hours pass, but eventually doctors agree I can go home, with supervision from Mum.*

*Mum takes it to the extreme, making me a bed on their bedroom floor. I don't think she sleeps, just watches me and my every move.*

*I feel guilty and tell her I'm sorry.*

*For the first time in years, mum speaks about Dad. She tells me she had been asleep, she woke up and Dad was not in bed. She looked for him in the house and noticed the car keys were gone. Looking out the letterbox she saw the car had gone also. She knew what he had gone to do. There was nothing she could do. Mum tried hard to help him. Made him appointments with the GPs, she had been concerned about his mental health and frame of mind. He didn't attend the appointments. She had called the police, they arrived to inform her a body had been found by a dog walker. It was our car. Mum already knew he was gone.*

*In a desperate emotional situation tonight, we found connection and honesty. Mum shared her hurt, her experience of his death with me. I found a new trust with mum in this conversation. Finally, I felt seen.*
*Mum trusted me and openly talk about it.*

*"I will not do this again" I reassure Mum.*

*"Get some sleep, I promise not to disappear in the night."*

*In this moment, Mum's love and concern is felt.*

*It is an extreme shift, from not knowing where I was, to not even being able to stand up without her panicking where I was going. I'm 16-years-old but feel like a toddler again.*
*I wonder, is she feeling like how I felt when she left a room after Dad died. Unsure if she would come back.*

*We try to giggle about it, "Mum I'm going for a wee… do you want to come with me?" I joke.*

148

*Our bond is coming back.*

*Mum's relationship with Him doesn't change, but our mother/daughter relationship does.*

*We hit a tough spot again when you tell us you are pregnant. We make our way through that.*

*When you have the second baby, I feel incredibly pushed out of the house because of the lack of space and that does poke at old wounds.*

*Our relationship goes from strength-to-strength once I don't live in the house. I'm happier without the stress and tension of feeling trapped in that house and environment.*
*Although I have difficulties in my relationships, Mum is always there on the end of the phone. Her time is full, working, a young family, but somehow, we find time for chats and quick visits to the shops. We make the best of the time we can grab.*

# Christmas 2012

I've not seen you much recently and you look tired, you have been working a lot of hours in the lead up to Christmas and you put it down to that.

I offer you a Baileys, you don't drink alcohol, but always have a Baileys at Christmas and your birthday.
"No thanks, I don't fancy one" you say
I offer you a coffee.
"No thanks" you reply
"I've been off some foods and drinks recently. Coffee is one of them."
This strike me as unusual you drink coffee in bucket loads, always.

You open up and tell me you have been feeling very tired and fed up. Really fed up, in fact you even speak about leaving Him and starting a new life.

"Let's try and enjoy Christmas, I will make an appointment with the doctor in the new year." you suggest.
We leave the conversation there and continue with Christmas.

I am worried, you never go to the doctors, thinking about it you have never been poorly really. You are one of the most laid back, unfazed people I've ever met. You always say to us if we come to you with a problem,

"Can you change the situation? Is there anything you can do about it?"

If we say no, you reply
"Well try not to worry and think about it too much. If you can't change it, then we just have to try move on."

*Our brains must be wired differently, I am an overthinker, things play on my mind and go round and round.*

*You, on the other hand seem to effortlessly say, "Oh well." and move on.*

*I'm sure that is not true, things must trouble you, but no-one around you would ever guess.*

*This is why Freddie Mercury's The Great Pretender is your song. It is always the one we catch you singing along to whilst washing up.*

*You always have a smile, a giggle and time for anyone that needs it.*
*You never burden us (as grown-up daughters) with your problems. Sure, we talk for hours and there is no topic we can't talk to you about. The only topic that ever feels too difficult is Dad.*
*In the early years you would not talk about him at all.*

*You must also feel abandoned and betrayed. I understand that it is too painful for you to talk about. Even with something as huge and life changing as that situation, you say "there isn't anything I can do about it, life moves on."*

*Too painful to even process.*

*As I get older, what once seemed like a way for you to cope, makes me realise the damage that not processing and talking about things does to a person. It lays dormant in us until eventually there is no other option but to address it. By refusing to acknowledge the situation you prevent healing from taking place.*
*By simply trying to pretend it doesn't exist or it didn't happen, doesn't heal the wound. However, this is generational behaviour.*

*Behaviours that are taught to us and we don't know to question as we grow up.*

*You change back to your maiden name eventually after Dad died. Originally, I found it strange, I wonder is it about claiming your own identity back moving forward. You aren't Dad's wife, you are his widow. That must be tricky to explain to people when giving your married name.*

*In January 2013, I wake up from an emergency C-section, having had a general anaesthetic.*

*The first person I call is Mum, my voice still croaky and weird, I tell you Harleigh has arrived. He was starting to open my scar from the last C-section from the inside, they had to get him out fast.*

*"I'm still worrying about you Mum, are you okay?"*

*You reply, "Don't worry about me right now, you get some rest. I can't wait to meet him."*

*I'm kept in hospital over the weekend, you said you were tired and would see us when we get home.*

*This is so unlike you, you have been so excited, I know how much you wanted to come and have a cuddle. I'm really worried about this tiredness now.*

*We come home on Sunday and Izzy has made us dinner, so I don't have to cook. We finish eating as Izzy goes to the kitchen to take a call.*

*She returns in the room and looks concerned. A serious expression on her face. Moments ago, we were celebrating the safe arrival of the baby.*

*"What's happened? Who was that?" I ask.*

*"It is Mum, the doctors have sent her to hospital." Izzy explains, "She needs me to take some things for her. I am sorry Mad, I'm going to have to go."*

*The next few days are a blur, trying to rest and recover, each time Mum calls there is more confusion.*

*The gallbladder is fine, it isn't kidney stones. Blood tests have high readings for something the doctors are concerned about.*

*More scans are arranged, you must stay in hospital until they get to what the problem is.*

*We chat on the phone, I'm desperate to come and see you, but you with your mum head on you say no.*

*You don't want me to bring Harleigh into another hospital, you want to meet him at home. Izzy spends a lot of time with you, playing cards and keeping you company. It is a comfort to know that if it cannot be me, you have Izzy.*

*Finally, after a week, you ring and say you are being discharged.*

*"What have they said? Do they know what is happening?" I ask, in search for answers.*

*"I will talk to you when I get to yours." that is all you say.*

153

*I have a sinking feeling this isn't good news.*

*Izzy collects you and, sure enough, you come straight to mine.*

*I notice how jaundiced you are, the visible weight loss. You look tired and vulnerable.*

*Holding Harleigh for the first time, it should have been a joyous moment. Instead, you must tell me the doctors think you have cancer. From my nursing days I know that they would not tell you this unless they are sure.*

*The doctors are waiting for some more results and further tests need to be done. They have said that your pancreas is enlarged. That is what they are concerned about.*

*Tears start to flow, eventually turning to sobs, I am hormonal from giving birth a week ago. I'm tired from nursing a newborn. Emotions flood through my body and none of it feels real. My beautiful baby boy in the arms of my Mum who is so poorly.*

*I lay in bed that night and tell Leigh, I think Mum is going to die. He reassures me and says not to jump to the worst-case scenario. I was a nurse, I know pancreatic cancer is known as the silent killer, it doesn't show symptoms until it's too late.*

*Over the next 6 weeks, there are tests and appointments at the hospital. I still can't drive from the C-section and Mum encourages me to rest. I'm breastfeeding Harleigh, Mum tells me I must eat, to feed him. It's such a pull of emotions, I don't feel like eating or doing anything, but I know I must look after me to be able to feed Harleigh and take care of Mikayla.*

154

*Our worst fears are confirmed, it is pancreatic cancer. The doctors say they never thought it would be that, given you are 47-years-old and otherwise fit and healthy. Our glimmer of hope is that because you are young, fit and healthy they want to proceed with surgery. The Whipple Procedure. It is a huge operation and will need to be done in a London hospital.*

*I stay in a hotel nearby, Charley and Izzy decide they are coming too. I need to be near you, Mum. I need to know I can get to you if there are complications. It's not ideal with a 6-week-old baby, but this is my way of coping.*

*The operation will take between 10–12 hours. We walk into the pre-operation ward the morning of your surgery, you go and get your gown on whilst us three girls and Harleigh wait for you. A nurse from reception approaches me and informs me I should not have a baby here; they advise that he should not be in the hospital. I break down, we shouldn't be here, Mum shouldn't be here, none of this should be happening. She's my mum and I need to be here with her. My baby is 6-weeks-old, he needs me. It's an impossible situation to be in.*
*The nurse sympathetically smiles and nods, "I understand."*
*They don't ask us to leave.*
*Mum returns, gown on and ready to go into surgery, she asks if we should just forget about the operation and go for breakfast.*
*Her way of coping.*
*She doesn't really want the surgery but wants to do all she can to stay alive. She doesn't want to leave us; she doesn't want to die. We watch as she is wheeled to theatre,*
*never have I prayed so hard that this is all going to be okay.*

*Lost, us three sisters walk back to the hotel room, sit in our room for the day reminiscing on our childhood, the good and the bad. We bond over the turmoil we are all feeling. The tragedy we have lived through with Dad and how it has always left us needing Mum.*

*"She is our person, our security blanket in life."*

*Our adult to always turn to. None of us can comprehend a life with her gone. We wait for the call from the hospital. Later in the evening it comes.*
*The nurse from the recovery ward tells us Mum is in the recovery room. The consultants would like us to go to the hospital to talk with them.*

*Charley remains down in the main waiting area with Harleigh, whilst Izzy and I make our way to the recovery suite.*
*Even having worked in hospital environments, it still shocks me to see Mum this vulnerable. Tubes up her nose, equipment attached to her everywhere. The nurse takes us to her bedside and explains she will call the consultant to inform him we have arrived.*

*"Everything go okay? Is she okay?" I ask the nurse, longing to hear a reassuring yes.*

*It does not come, she gives me a knowing look and gently says, "The consultant will talk with you."*

*My heart breaks in this moment.*

*They haven't been able to say yes it has gone okay. I know the news we are going to receive is bad.*

*Ushered into a side room, on a little sofa Izzy and I wait silently for the consultant to talk.*

*"We are sorry, we were unable to remove the cancer, its attached to an artery. We didn't expect this to be the case. We have removed a lot of her bowel; this gives the cancer room to grow. It will give your mum a bit more time."*

*"Thank you for trying and doing all you could, we appreciate it. I know you must hear it all the time, but she doesn't deserve this. No one deserves this. She is 47-years-old, with six children and two grandchildren. One is just a baby downstairs. She has so much life left to live." I say in pure disbelief.*

*Both doctors have tears in their eyes, it must be the hardest part of their jobs to deliver this type of news.*

*Sitting on the sofa in this little side room, that familiar old feeling returns.*

*My head under water, I can't quite hear what is being said.*
*Thoughts rushing through my mind.*
*My heart aches.*
*A longing to run away, run away from this pain. Having completely no idea how we will cope.*

*How she will cope.*

*"What will we do without her?"*

*She can't leave, even as an adult a sense of abandonment creeps in, I want to rush to her side and beg for her not to leave us.*

*I'm back feeling like that lost 11-year-old girl. Longing for comfort and security. A way of making this stop.*
*I didn't expect these old emotions and insecurities about life to resurface as an adult.*

*I had never allowed myself to think of a life without Mum.*

*I thought things like this would feel different as an adult.*
*It doesn't, I feel my vulnerable inner child return.*

*The confusion so strong, as a child that faced the sudden loss of a parent for it always to hurt that there was no warning. It just happened and that was it.*
*To an adult now having to watch my other parent die so young of cancer.*
*Life at this point seems incredibly cruel and unfair.*

*Mum still isn't awake properly, it is late and we have to find Charley to tell what we have been told.*
*Back in the hotel room tonight I am reminded, of that childhood feeling, being grateful of not being alone.*
*Us three sisters agree to rest on the news tonight, knowing tomorrow we will have to break the news to others.*

*Each time Harleigh wakes for a feed in the night, we can all be heard quietly sobbing.*

*The child-like feeling still with me, I see Mum awake for the first time after her surgery.*
*All I can do is lay my head on her chest, listen to her heartbeat, and feel the comfort in the smell of Mum.*
*Nothing and no-one will ever replace this feeling.*

*The hospital equipment beeping, staff doing their duties, the busy London world continuing outside the window.*
*We share this moment, comforting each other, in silence, knowing nothing is ever going to be the same.*

*The doctors suggest chemotherapy after the operation and Mum agrees to have this. We let you know we will support you in whatever decision you make.*
*If you want to, then we will do all we can to support you, but equally we know this treatment cannot save you.*
*If you decide not to have it, that is also your choice.*
*The doctors predict you will have about 12 months to live.*
*We make the most of the time we have left together when you are feeling well enough. We make memories and of course have all our weddings.*

*The hardest part of the situation is you are now married to Him, the Macmillan team had suggested this, for some reason you follow their advice.*
*It means he is your next of kin.*
*Coming to see you at home when you are so poorly is difficult for us all.*
*We don't have keys to the house. We are not permitted to have those now we don't live there.*
*Even if we did the door is locked from the inside.*
*We fear once we leave the house, we will not be able to get back in to see you.*
*The nurses have set up a hospital bed for you at home and we take it in turns to tag team so that we know we can get back into the house to see you.*

*No-one should have this added stress when a loved one is dying.*

*We take care of you the best we can. Once you start to become agitated and confused, we know it is time to talk to the nurses about you moving to the hospice.*

*He is not happy when I mention our concerns to the palliative care team.*

*Having worked in nursing homes and within palliative care, I am aware that you being at home for your final weeks will be difficult. We have open mother and daughter conversations about your death.*
*We have already planned and spoken with the nursing team, that if your care becomes too difficult to manage at home you will go to the hospice.*

*Mindful your children are so young still.*

*When the ambulance team arrive to collect you, He has an appointment to go to.*
*I can't understand why anything else is more important, than being with mum as she is transferred to the hospice.*
*But we are used to this with him.*
*It confirms my feelings about Him from childhood and nothing has changed, even as you are dying.*

*I watch as the ambulance team takes you out of our family home for the last time.*
*You are unable to speak now but I let you know I am here and am not going to leave you.*
*I join you in the ambulance for the short journey to the hospice and relief fills my body.*

*The tears flow as you are now going to get the best care, in a quiet, calm environment. A place we are welcome in and can freely visit. No more fear of being locked out or unable to see you.*

*The hospice is tranquil and full of amazing staff. They make you comfortable and we stay with you all the time.*
*In the 5 days you are there, we have space, time, and peace.*
*To begin to come to terms with what is happening.*
*It is sad we couldn't feel this in your own home.*

*We play Freddie Mercury's music in the background, with a sense of being close to you. The evening you took your final breaths, our Aunt, Izzy and I are by your side.*

*Holding your hand as you look at me for the final time.*
*My comfort is that you are free from pain, not just the physical pain you have endured in the last year, but the emotional pain you carried for all these years.*

*I hope Dad is there waiting for you, to be reunited again and I can't help a small smile wondering if you are giving him what-for as you meet again.*

*I genuinely have no clue how we will carry on without you.*
*Without your love, hugs and giggles.*

*There is an overwhelming relief that your relationship with Him is over.*
*We no longer have to live on eggshells.*

*Not only are you free, but we are free also.*

*How I wish it could be under a different circumstance.*

*Feelings I had in childhood about Him were not validated. Those instincts had been right, and I had been powerless. No-one had listened.*

*Izzy and I arrive at the funeral home, the women look at us confused, they only know you are married with three young children.*

*No mention of us three older daughters.*

*The day of your funeral is intense. We are not your next of kin so have little input to funeral plans.*

*We inform them of the songs you want but one of those is changed.*
*I am able to do a reading,*
*Maybe people start to understand the situation when they are invited to a wake, we know nothing about.*
*Finally, people see the way we are treated.*
*It Is too late by now; we have had a lifetime of it.*

*It takes us a year to get some of your ashes, but eventually we do. We fulfil your final wish, to have them put in a firework.*

*I thought you were joking when you first told us, but you weren't.*

*We take the firework to the village hall where we spent many happy childhood memories and let it off there.*

*It is special and feels like our final goodbye, in a place that will always mean so much.*

## *Things to consider*

- Children have intuition and have a right to those feelings being heard.

- Dads sudden death was the traumatic event, but the lack of support after has impacted the years of unhealed trauma.

- The impact of invalidation and harm caused by the man introduced after Dad's death caused irreversible trauma.

- Consideration of the child's feelings about any person they feel replaces the parent they lost to suicide.

- Their feelings matter.

- Their feelings are valid.

- Their feelings need to be heard.

## *Parenting with friendship*

We all have an idea, and our own opinions of what parenting should look like. There is also a heavy societal idea of what parents should be.

When Mikayla came along, I joked that when you have a baby you should get an instruction manual on the child you have grown and given birth to. I don't mean a general parenting book, there are countless books on the parenting of newborns/children/teens.

What I mean is for this individual child. In hindsight, one of the things I wish I had been encouraged to do more was to follow my own mothering instinct.

The best example in our situation was "Let them cry it out."

"Don't always pick up and comfort them, let them settle and self soothe."

Because of my own childhood being the way it was, I guess there weren't many parenting skills for me to learn, other than survival skills. How to somehow look after and protect myself the best way I could.

I was desperate to get parenting right.

Mikayla, for the first 18 months of her life, was a crier. She cried a lot, day and night. Mainly the nights, she took sleepless nights to the next level.

My instincts told me to hold her, pick her up, cuddle her. The books and 'professionals' told me not to do this all the time.

Leaving her to cry didn't work, repeatedly the health visitors told me she would learn and that babies wont cry for long periods of time and will learn to self-soothe and fall asleep.

Mikayla didn't. The more I left her to cry the more stressful the whole situation became.

Then I was told to try keep myself busy, by washing up or putting headphones on and distract myself from her noise. To remain calm.

I did think at the time, "That is easy for you to advise, when you are not the one listening to the crying."

In a desperate bid to be a good parent in society/professionals' eyes, I continued to go against my instincts and followed the advice. What did I know about parenting? I was brand new to this, the professionals knew how to parent, they must be right I thought.

Let me tell you, I regret this heavily to this day. The advice/guidance I really needed was follow your instincts and someone who could hold space for me to listen to how I was struggling and reassure me that it would be okay.

I also remember a conversation with a health visitor about breastfeeding. My instinct was to feed on demand and Mikayla did a lot of demanding. Much of the time it was for comfort, I didn't mind, I also found comfort and relief in the fact when we were nursing, she wasn't crying. I felt I was at least getting something right. Again, advice was to not always feed her and to time some of her feeds similar to how bottle-fed babies have a schedule.

This also went against my motherly instinct. I spoke to the health visitor about nature and instincts, in the way that a cat for example doesn't look at a clock and tell her kittens, "It is not time to be fed."

My instinct was to also co-sleep. With cats in mind again, my example was that they don't leave their kittens in a room to cry, they all snuggle warm together with the kitten's content and safe, their mother with them. I questioned why does society have this massive issue with children being taught/forced to sleep in their own room almost from day one of their lives?

"Because they need to learn to sleep alone and avoid attachment issues." But surely those things come after a child grows and feels loved and safe? Being loved and feeling safe with their parents and the home environment.

Plus, we only have one short life any way and in the end we all die. Is a baby/childhood not the one precious time we should have filled with all the love and cuddles we can get?

Things were different when Harleigh was born, it was my second time around and this parenting wasn't all new to me. In the first week of his life, my Mum was diagnosed with terminal cancer. No words will ever describe the two extreme emotions, to have a healthy beautiful baby boy and to watch as your Mum's health deteriorates and dies. This time it was all about the cuddles and nursing. It was my comfort to the pain, and it was his comfort when he cried. I followed my instincts and quite frankly at this point couldn't care less about what others thought of my parenting style. It's not a situation I would wish on anyone, and once more, it brought the cruel fact of life and death back to my world.

Harleigh was a different baby, he was calm, content, and happy. Was that because he was a different child, maybe? Was that because I met his needs, didn't allow him to cry it out, because I followed my instincts and was calmer and more confident? I will never know, but it brought more regret that I hadn't parented Mikayla as a baby that way.

My parenting really came under judgement once more for the years that followed when Harleigh was diagnosed autistic and with ADHD aged 6. In the years that followed this, I once again found myself frantically searching how to parent him and meet his needs.

Once again much of what I was advised and the strategies we put in place didn't work. I will admit this caused a lot of frustration, stress and unnecessary harm to all of us as a family.

When I found the autistic online community and adults with lived experience, things changed for us.

I learned from those with lived experience, those who understood a different type of parenting. These were my people, the ones I was desperate to connect with and learn from. Those who empowered me to listen to my instincts and in learning/listening and trusting in getting to know Harleigh's unique needs, I could tune in once more to parenting, but follow my instincts rather than do what others think parenting him should look like. Although strategies they had suggested I tried were for autistic children, they did not work to support

Harleigh. I then learned about pathological demand avoidance (PDA), a profile of autism that needs a vastly different approach to parenting.

The most crucial thing I learned was about anxiety levels and the need to feel in control to lessen the anxiety.

This was a huge lightbulb moment and through deeper learning about Harleigh's diagnosis, I didn't just read and think I understand this, I read and thought wow this describes me. My life experiences and difficulties. From connecting with other parents this seems to be quite a common experience. Lots of life experiences started to make sense. (I am on the pathway for assessment for autism/ADHD, but that's a story for another time)

The reason I mention this, is because it was a big turning point in my connection with Harleigh and my parenting style.

I sat and thought about childhood from my perspective and from Harleigh's with the things he has difficulties with. This led me to thinking of the type of parenting I needed and how this might be similar for my children.

I've talked about the feeling of things being out of my control in childhood. The way this made me feel unsafe and that I wasn't being seen/heard/validated.

How I longed to feel I had some kind of control and stability in my life.

As much as I needed Mum to be a parent, what I also wanted was the feeling of being her friend. When friendships don't come easy and you feel alone, a friend at home would have brought comfort.

I started to change the parenting of my own children.

To be a friend, someone they feel confident and comfortable talking to.

To be someone they want to talk to and know they will be heard.

To validate their thoughts and feelings.

Guide them through making their own decisions.

Compromising.

Explaining why things need to be done/not done.

Making plans about what we are doing together.

Lowering demands.

Giving them choices.

Involving them in decision-making.

Reminding them I'm here if/when they need me.

Respecting their need for their own space/time.

Embracing our differences with acceptance for one another. Apologising when I should (I am human too, I/we don't always get things right and its okay to show children this).

Modelling and growing together; explaining why I think I've got something wrong, not excusing the behaviour simply because I'm an adult.

Connecting with them through their interests and hobbies.

Parenting with friendship doesn't stop me from being a parent. It doesn't stop me from teaching and modelling parenting. It doesn't mean I'm not the adult who is responsible. It doesn't mean I don't care or just let them do whatever they please.

We have boundaries and they understand why they are in place for safety and being mindful of each other's needs.

I've been criticised many times, when people say,

"You allow them far too much control, they control you and they need to have discipline."

This is where I explain that this for me is the beauty in parenting with friendship.

I allow them to feel in control by communicating and listening to their needs.

Allowing them to feel in control is not the same as them being in control.

I am still the parent. I am still the responsible adult, but I am supporting them in making choices that they feel comfortable with. We talk about actions/reactions possible outcomes from the decisions they make, the positive and negative. It guides them to learn and practice making informed decisions. It allows them to advocate for themselves and have a voice. It allows them to explore feelings of anxiety and worry with me and find ways I can support them or ways they can support themselves. It allows them to know it's okay and safe to tell me when they don't feel comfortable doing something and the why, so we can problem-solve together.

I am proud of all my children. I'm proud to be their parent, but I'm also very privileged that they consider me a friend and a person they can turn to with their worries and concerns.

In parenting with friendship, I will always firstly and mainly be their parent, to love and protect them. To support them to grow and guide them through life the best way I can.

What a beautiful gift to know you always have a friend too.

We learn parenting from our parents; the good, the bad, and everything in between. Some of us don't have many parenting skills to learn from.

It's okay to break your parents' traditions if they don't feel right to you and your children.

It's okay to make new parenting styles.

It's okay to be the changes you want to see be passed down to the next generation.

It's okay to not get it right and to say sorry.

It's okay to throw out the traditional parenting book.

It's okay to follow your instinct and to take the lead from your child.

It's okay to realise that when a child is grieving from the loss of a parent to suicide (and any other grief), they, and you, may need a different parent/child relationship.

## *Things to consider*

- This is my personal interpretation of my own parenting based on what I needed as a child and how I parent my own children.

- There is work on trauma-informed parenting.

- I would recommend researching and learning about trauma-informed parenting.

# Five C's to consider when supporting a child who is grieving a loss to suicide

- Compassion
    - Validate their feelings and reassure them that it is okay to feel confused about emotions.

- Care
    - Lots of care to ensure they feel worthy of love after the abandonment.

- Connection
    - Parenting with compassion and friendship. Hold space with a desire to support healing together.

- Consistency
    - Gentle consistency of holding space and offering to listen.

- Conversation
    - Open and honest communication. Answering their questions and share their confusion.

## *Five things to forgive*

Reflecting on my childhood, looking deeper and closer at the events that have remained in my head for many years has given me the opportunity to think about how to release emotions and to heal. Part of this has come from being open and allowing my inner child to tell her story and relive memories. It brought back the intense feeling of isolation that was always present. Much of what is written in this book, I've not discussed with anyone before. Writing it down has helped me to heal, I could read the words back and look at my inner child's perspective from my adult viewpoint. I wanted to find a way to release these emotions and recover from the traumatic events. I always held on to them, fearing that letting them go would mean letting the memory of Dad go. Holding on to these memories I thought was the only way to keep his memory alive, now I understand processing and sharing these painful thoughts, I can let go of them and remember the happy times. I come to find there were five things that I needed to forgive, not for other people, but for myself. Forgiving these things has brought me a sense of healing and a lighter feeling. I no longer carrying these feelings with nowhere for them to go.

1.      Forgiveness for the adults who didn't come to my rescue.

As a child, the longing to be rescued was real. For an adult to sweep you up and take you to a safe place where you could be cared for and loved. Where they could listen to your thoughts and feelings. A person and place where you felt understood and accepted. For someone to see things from your perspective and see how hard this situation was. Why didn't they come? Why didn't this happen? As time passed, it become normal life and the older you get the more you realise that people no longer see you as a child that needs support. Didn't they care? Were you forgotten? Out of sight and no-one else's responsibility?

When the unexpected happens, people don't know how to react or what to do for the best. Maybe people thought we were okay? Maybe they didn't think it was their place to swoop in and support?

I carried around resentment for other adults' abandonment. Once I was able to see this, I saw that the only person this was hurting was me. Holding on to frustration for those adults didn't affect them. They didn't even know or have an awareness of that. Why do we hold on to those feelings? What purpose do they serve?

In truth, they fester and take over our rational thoughts. They feed into our feelings of being unworthy and not wanted. Not good enough for love. We are seeking our own self-worth based on the actions of others. This in turn leads to an unhealthy feeling of not being good enough.

Realising that this is not to be taken personally allowed the opportunity to believe in self-worth. That is hard to establish as a child when it isn't felt.

Those adults didn't know the full situation. They didn't know what was needed, as I couldn't vocalise it. They had lives of their own, families and other responsibilities. As an adult I've been able to use that voice, some of those adults have apologised and admitted that they didn't know what to do.

It was never about the apologies for me, it was simply part of healing and to let go of the negative feelings around this that I carried from childhood.

Forgiving them has created space within myself. It has freed me of those feelings.

I do this for my own growth.

2.    Forgiving, validating and seeing my inner child's experience.

Writing, processing and exploring my inner child's experience has enabled me to hold space for my inner child. It seems strange now, that this experience has belonged only in my memory. I've never truly allowed time and space to sit with all the emotions, how it all affected most of my life. I've tried to push past it, tried to forget about, at times even denied it happened. When we don't have the opportunities and skills to do this growing up, it becomes something that others think you have simply gotten over. You start to believe those things too and think it was all in the past, its gone, there is no fixing it.

As I said in the introduction, learning to feel the pain, connect to the emotions and sit with the difficult thoughts, has helped support releasing those frustrations.

I've never allowed myself this time before, part of that has been I knew it wouldn't be a quick process. I also felt that once I started this, I needed to be ready to commit to the work that goes into healing. This last year of writing I've allowed my inner child that time and space. Writing chapters and then giving time to process after.

Self-validation has been freeing. To be able to acknowledge this was a traumatic experience for a child to go through. Understanding it was okay that as a child I didn't know how to grieve. I didn't know how to use my voice. I didn't want to feel a burden to others. Possibly this could have been supported by a professional over the years, or as a child, had I had therapy and known it was somebody's job to support and listen.

Looking back, I think there could have been a benefit to having therapy, I think children need a person and space to freely express the difficulties in grieving after a parental suicide.

There is something powerful in being able to forgive our inner child. Forgive them for struggling and being so hard on themselves. Being able to say to your younger self, "I forgive you and I'm proud of you."

3.      Forgiveness for Dad and the abandonment.

Forgiveness for the person that has died by suicide is a very personal thing. As with all types of forgiveness, it can't be forced, it simply has to be something we feel, that comes when it is ready. I don't believe there is any time limit on this and there certainly shouldn't be any judgment on how long (if ever) this takes. Some people I have spoken to said they forgave him straight away; they knew he wasn't well. Maybe that can happen for adults, with fully developed brain and life experience to understand this. As a child there wasn't this real understanding to the concept. Yes, I could understand that he didn't feel well in his mind, but the concept that he took his own life and left us just didn't make sense. As a child we have an idea that when some someone is unwell, they can see a doctor, take medicine and get better. The lack of knowledge that this isn't always possible with mental illness, it is far more complex, it is a lot for a child's brain to process.

Some people might think it is excessive that I haven't been able to say I forgive him for 30 years. Part of that is in not having the support and skills to grieve his death. I realise I haven't been able to forgive because I hadn't grieved and had not developed the skills to do so. I find it interesting as an adult now, when adults talk of the difficulties they have with suicide grief. How complex and different it is to be grieving for a person that dies of natural causes.

If adults find it so confusing, how can children be expected to navigate these emotions without support. Adults find it hard to have conversations. As a child it was impossible to find other children to talk to about the enormity of the hurt and confusion.

I'm no longer ashamed to say it has taken 30 years to say I forgive Dad. It has taken this long because of the lifelong impact the feelings of abandonment brought. I'm not ashamed nor do I apologise for being a sensitive soul who feels things deeply.
It's always been said in such a negative way,

"You are too sensitive."

This was a life-changing traumatic event in childhood and the sheer devastation in its impact has contributed to the length of time that has taken for me to accept.

Writing has helped to make sense of the experience and processing has led to a natural forgiveness.

There is a definite lightness in saying, "I forgive you."

4.      Forgiveness for the parent left behind.

As an adult and a parent myself now, it's been easier to step back from the emotional situation and look at the experience from a different perspective. I can't begin to imagine the sadness and responsibility placed on the parent left behind to support and care for children left behind from suicide. On top of the grief and abandonment for your own loss of that loved one.

Being able to look at it through this perspective, I have found compassion for Mum being left in that situation. It must have been an impossible situation for her to find herself in.

That doesn't invalidate the feelings I had as a child. I needed to allow my inner child to have her voice, to validate how she felt let down and emotionally abandoned. Once I was able to hold space and pick apart why, as a child, I felt unseen and unsupported, I could also look at it from an adult perspective too.

The ache I had towards needing Mum and not having that connection with her growing up made sense. Being a child and needing a parent is normal. She had her own unprocessed traumas, I'm sure she did do her best. We are human, we make mistakes, we live and grow from our experiences. We all have regrets. It has been hard processing this part of childhood because she has passed away. I can't talk through these things with her. I can't ask her for the answers to the questions I have.

What I can do is validate my inner child's experience and say, yes, that was hard, but I believe not intentional.

Processing that naturally brought forgiveness for Mum. I couldn't feel that before as if I tried to forgive her it felt I was invalidating those feeling my inner child had felt.

A heaviness has been lifted, even though I can't say these words to Mum, I can feel it in my heart.

"I forgive you Mum."

5.      Forgiveness for a lack of self-worth.

I've never been able to be kind to my inner child, never appreciated all she did to help us survive. Never thanked her for doing her best. Without her I wouldn't be here or who I am today.

Something from my Health and Social care courses struck a chord: Maslow's Hierarchy of Needs[4]. Maslow proposed that the psychological needs are the most important of all human needs.

Needing the security and foundations to be able to achieve the higher potential in life. My sisters and I didn't have that. We didn't get those foundations to build self-worth and security.

---

[4] Maslow, A. H. (1943). A theory of human motivation. Psychological Review, 50(4), 370–396.

This is what I really hope to highlight. The need for children to have those foundations secured from adults around them, to reach their full potential.

## *30-year anniversary*

Walking through the heavy gates, probably still the originals. A place where time stands still, the cemetery. It could be 30 years ago, the only thing that's really changed is there are more graves. More souls that have departed this earth and maybe left a story untold.

Sometimes, it feels a lifetime ago, a whole different life. Sometimes, it still feels like yesterday.
I didn't expect this 30 years later.
Can any of us really know what to expect the future to hold or how our grief will change over the years? I doubt it. Sometimes, maybe it would be nice, to know the future, the happy times, to know our lives will continue. Life is full of ups and downs, happy and sad experiences. The unpredictability is what makes it life, I guess. Somehow, we find the hope and trust that life will be enjoyable again. Most of the people buried here, would want us, the living, their loved ones, to live a full and happy life. It takes time for that to feel possible again. Eventually memories become less painful and can be smiled at and thought of fondly.

The pigeons gently coo as they always do. A bunch of roses in one hand and a full watering can in the other, I sit down at your grave once more.

"How has it been 30 years, Dad?"

It looks clean all tidied up. We did a good job, together making it look nice again.

I hear children in the distance playing. Looking over to where I sat all those years ago as a little girl, you can't see the playground now. Trees and bushes have grown, I feel how much nicer that is. For families visiting graves of loved ones, but also for those children playing. Not looking at a cemetery as they run around at play times.

All the dandelions gently blowing in the wind catch my attention. I lean over and pick one.

Remembering how I had picked them and wished for your return as a little girl.

What would I wish for now, 30 years on?

"A wish that you could still be here."

"A wish that I could go back in time and know the things I know now?"

A wish I could go back and tell that hurt little girl what her future holds?...

"A chance to whisper that it is going to be okay."

"Tell her how worthy of love she is."

"Remind her, she is strong and has wonderful achievements to come."

"Let her know, her worth doesn't come from those around her, but in the way she views herself."

"Reassure her she isn't too sensitive; she has a big heart and feels the emotions deeply. And that's okay."

"Be mindful to whom you give your love, care and attention, you need that the most for your healing."

"You may feel different and misunderstood much of the time, but there are people out there who understand, and the connection will be amazing once you find them."

"It's okay to say when you feel unsafe and confused."

"It's okay to set those emotions and pain free."

"It's okay to talk about your feelings. It's okay to admit when they feel too much."

"Some days will feel too much, be gentle with yourself."

"Rest and know that this is all a lot."

"On the days that hurt, and the tears come, let them flow. Know there will be days when it hurts a little less. Days/weeks/years are unpredictable, they come and go. It's all part of grieving."

"This wasn't your fault."

"One day, you will tell your story, share your insight and use your voice to help other children like you."

"You will be a mother who strives to be the generational change."

"You will find your place and purpose."

185

"You will find your dreams and have the strength to follow them."

"You are enough for simply being you."

"One day you will be the change you want to see in the world."

I pick five dandelions.

This time, I don't blow them making wishes.

This time I blow each one and blow away the forgive you.

1.  I forgive the adults who didn't come to my rescue.
2.  I forgive my inner child, I'm sorry for always being so harsh on you.
3.  I forgive you, Dad, and the feeling of abandonment.
4.  I forgive you, Mum, the parent left behind to deal with the hurt.
5.  I forgive myself for not having compassion and self-worth.

A sense of calmness washes over me.
A stillness I've not experienced sitting here before.

I visualise that little girl who sat here all those years ago.
I imagine smiling at her.

"I've listened to you."

"I've given you the voice you have always longed to use."

"I've seen you."

"We become the adult we needed. It has taken so many years, but we have got here together."

"You don't have to live inside that space with all those boxes of memories. You don't need to hold on to all those emotions and feelings anymore."

"You are free."

I picture her freedom to be with the parents she lost as a child. Of course, my inner child will always live in me, she is me and I am her, but I've set free the lost and broken little girl.

So, Dad, I smile, I feel ready to turn the page, a new chapter of my life. A 41-year-old woman, a mother, a wife, a friend, without the heaviness of all the past.

I've long wondered what the purpose was, why this all happened.

Maybe this book was part of the purpose.

To use a voice and share the insight which may benefit others. To bring hope and lessen the isolation for those experiencing this loss.

You will never be forgotten, and I miss you. I will always wonder the whys and how life could have been different. I've made peace with the fact that we will never know.

That's just what happened.

I hadn't realised before how my unhealed past had affected my parenting. The way grief took up such a space in me. How, on some level, it stopped me being available to fully connect with my own children.

It's time, Dad, for me to focus on my children, my connections with them, for the first time I feel I have the capacity to leave the past behind.

That tornado in my head is gone.
The boxes in the space in my head no longer have dust on.
They have been searched through until they make sense, sorted back into neat little boxes.

Walking away from the cemetery, I smile and think what an incredible journey this has been.

It doesn't end here.

The next stage is continuing to find ways to care for myself, maybe even therapy.

The experience will be lifelong, but healing my inner child has been a huge part of the process.

One of the changes we made as a family is with dandelions and wishes.
To find a way of connecting and understanding what the children might be wishing for, we say if you want to you don't have to keep it a secret you can share.

I might not be able to make your wish come true, but maybe we can try.

On Vinnie's first try, he grins and smiles, telling me he wishes for a yellow Lamborghini. I can't make that come true…. But we did spend his pocket money and bought a toy remote control car one. He was thrilled.

It's a way we have found to connect.

1994         2024

## *Final thoughts*

If you have made it through this book, thank you.

Thank you for also being part of this journey.

I hope you can take something from this to help your own healing journey.

My conclusions of my experience:

There is a big difference in grieving a parent to a natural death versus to a death by suicide.

I found acceptance for Mum's natural death much quicker.

Death by suicide has taken much longer to accept.

It's been a different grief journey.

Although I have found acceptance there will always be an element of

"Why?" and "What if?"

It wasn't Dad's death that caused the trauma. . .

It was the lack of support and not feeling seen or validated in my childhood grief.

Childhood trauma and loss continues into adulthood.
It's a grief and an experience we carry for our entire life.
I cannot highlight enough the importance of connection with others that have experienced this complex grief.

In childhood, if that isn't possible with another child, then crucial with a trusted adult.

In adulthood, with support groups, friends and family who can share our experiences and talk openly about our feelings.

This has been life changing for me to connect to others and lessen the isolation I carried.

We are not alone.

Sadly, there are many of us who have suffered this type of tragedy, and we need each other.

Don't give up hope in the darker times, there are happy memories to be made in life. Although it doesn't always feel like it, the ups and downs do have a way of balancing each other out eventually.

Over 30 years I never believed that one day I could be free of this grief and confusion, but I've found a way and now look to the future with excitement of where life might lead me.

The opportunities that might come my way.

For the first time, I don't feel that I'm just existing … I want to start living.

I hope you find that too one day.

Maddie x

# Charities and support organisations.

There are some incredible charities and support organisations out there, where you can find information, guidance and support.

ANDYSMANCLUB
Run peer-to-peer support groups for men over 18 going through storms in their lives, every Monday at 7pm excluding bank holidays. Groups are free to attend with no registration required.
The group was founded after the death by suicide of Andy Roberts. Andy gave no indication to his family that he was suicidal, as a result, his brother-in-law, Luke Ambler, and mother, Elaine Roberts, founded ANDYSMANCLUB in the hope that men who struggled to open up had a safe space to do so.
To find out more,
email info@andysmanclub.co.uk
or head to www.andysmanclub.co.uk

PAPYRUS
Prevention of Young Suicide is the UK charity dedicated to the prevention of suicide and the promotion of positive mental health and emotional wellbeing in young people. Suicide is the biggest killer of people aged 35 and under in the UK.
PAPYRUS believes that many suicides are preventable.
PAPYRUS works with communities across the UK, engaging them in the mission to prevent suicide in children and young people – through resources, training, learning with them, and galvanising them to help save young lives. PAPYRUS offers a broad range of suicide prevention training, along with volunteering opportunities.
To learn more please visit: www.papyrus-uk.org

HOPELINE247

A 24-hour suicide prevention helpline provided by PAPYRUS Prevention of Young Suicide. HOPELINE247 is staffed by trained suicide prevention advisers, who work with young people – and anybody concerned for a young person – to help keep them safe from suicide. HOPELINE247 is a free and confidential call, text, and email service, which is available 24 hours a day, every day of the year (weekends and bank holidays included).

Call: 0800 068 4141

Text: 88247

Email: pat@papyrus-uk.org

CHILD BEREAVMENT UK

Helps children and young people (up to age 25), parents, and families, to rebuild their lives when a child grieves or when a child dies. The charity also provides training to professionals, equipping them to provide the best possible care to bereaved families.

Helpline: 0800 02 888 40

helpline@childbereavementuk.org

Live Chat via the website

www.childbereavementuk.org

WINSTONS WISH

Is a charity that helps children, teenagers and young adults (up to the age of 25) find their feet when their worlds are turned upside down by grief. Please call our freephone helpline team on 08088 020 021, Winstonswish.org (8am-8pm, weekdays) or email ask@winstonswish.org

HUB OF HOPE.
Mental Health support network.
Hubofhope.co.uk
SUICIDE BEREAVMENT SUPPORT UK
www.facebook.com
https://www.facebook.com/groups/161503584443512

MIND
Mind.org.uk
Mind Infoline- 0300 123 3393 (open 9am-6pm Monday-
Friday)

CRUSE BEREVEMENT SUPPORT
Cruse.org.uk
Helpline 0808 808 1677

SURVIVORS OF BEREAVEMENT BY SUICIDE
Uksobs.com
Call for support 0300 111 5065

SUPPORT AFTER SUICIDE PARTNERSHIP
Supportaftersuicide.org.uk

YOUNGMINDS
Youngminds.org.uk

CHILDLINE
0800 1111

SHOUT
www.giveusashout.org
Text SHOUT to 85258

THE SAMARITANS
116123

# Acknowledgements

People I would like to give a special thank you to, the book would not be what it is without your love support and encouragement.

You all have a special place in my heart.

My sisters - love you always.

Claire - the first person to read and help with editing and cheering me on from that first read.

Lisa - endless support at the end of a the phone, reading and editing until it must have sent you crazy.

Sabrina - my beautiful friend that just always believes in me and has supported with reading and editing.

Rachel - thank you for working with me to produce a beautiful cover and the endless formatting.

Jodie, George, Carrie and Sam - my friends who love me for me, love you millions.

Auntie Jay and Auntie Chris - thank you for all your love, support and understanding.

Paula, Linzi, Rachel, Harry, Steph and Kerri - Your words of support and encouragement have kept me going.

ANDYMAN CLUB - for supporting my book and Lucas for the comforting virtual hand hold and foreword.

Heidi- and our little affiliate group. Thank you for your support.

Sonia- for becoming a home from home for me and the children.

Authors and Co. - an amazing 'The One' book writing course. The book wouldn't be here without your guidance.

My Facebook friends - all those that have followed my writing journey, liked my posts and offered lovely words of encouragement and support. It has been amazing.

Piata - A friend I connected with on the book course. The first person I've truly connected to understanding this type of grief. This book would not be what it is without your love and support.

Nikki - For making the time to help and support with reading and editing.

Printed in Great Britain
by Amazon